SECOND LANGUAGE LEARNING
DATA ANALYSIS

Teachers' Manual

SECOND LANGUAGE LEARNING DATA ANALYSIS

Teachers' Manual

Susan Gass
Michigan State University

Antonella Sorace
University of Edinburgh

Larry Selinker
University of London, Birkbeck College

Routledge
Taylor & Francis Group
NEW YORK AND LONDON

First published by:

Lawrence Erlbaum Associates, Inc., Publishers
10 Industrial Avenue
Mahwah, New Jersey 07430

Reprinted 2010 by Routledge:

Routledge
Taylor & Francis Group
711 Third Avenue
New York, NY 10017

Routledge
Taylor & Francis Group
2 Park Square, Milton Park
Abingdon, Oxon OX14 4RN

ISBN 0-8058-3264-5

CONTENTS

INTRODUCTION

This Teacher's Manual, which accompanies the second edition of *Second Language Learning: Data Analysis,* provides suggested answers to the problems presented in the text. The goal of the text is to give students practice in analyzing data, by providing "hands-on" experience with actual second language data. From our first efforts in the early '80's we have learned that working with data is essential for anyone wishing to understand the processes involved in learning a second language. Our goal in the workbook has been to present data organized in such a way that by working through pedagogically organized problems, students are led to a discovery of theoretical and/or methodological issues. Our suggested answers here follow that ethos. We take the organized data from the workbook and provide worked through answers, in many cases from our own teaching, showing how data can be organized, reorganized and interrelated with other data and reanalyzed for the purposes of interpreting the data and drawing conclusions from them. All along, we have realized that argumentation in SLA is hard to teach and this has again motivated us highly here. Throughout this manual we have attempted to provide information on what counts as evidence for and against a particular analysis and how one can deal with real and putative counter-examples. In addition to the standard suggested answers, in many cases we have added three features new to this manual which we hope will add to its value: 1) an explicit statement of the purpose of the problem, 2) the source of the original data, and 3) suggested areas for additional discussion, this latter at times with additional references that can help the discussion. We hope that this information will help focus discussion as well as lead to in-depth work in the problem area where the teacher has the inclination and time.

Audio tapes are included with the Teacher's Manual. Instructors may make copies for students in the class. There are two parts to the audio tape: The first part is to be used as an accompaniment to some of the problems, the second part consists of additional data with suggestions that can be used for analysis. The first part provides a richness to the problem not available through written data (those problems that have taped material are indicated by a tape symbol). In some instances the tapes allow students to replicate original data; in other cases it allows them access to phonetic and phonological aspects of interlanguages that cannot be discerned through transcripts alone. In the second part of the audio tape are data sets unrelated to specific problems. We provide a description of the contents of this part of the tape as well as suggestions for ways to exploit these data. In the second part, the data are for the most part designed for students who are interested in the teaching and learning of languages other than English providing them with ample opportunities for interlanguage analyses of the language of interest.

In this Teacher's Manual, we hope we have helped teachers to help their students go from data to conclusions. We also hope that this exercise will enable students to think about what else they would like to know about these data and the subjects who produced them. Class time may often be devoted to ways in which one can empirically research in a more conclusive fashion the conclusions the students have come to. Finally, the problems in the workbook have been drawn from several sources, most notably the published literature. Concerning the work of our colleagues, in many cases this task to provide our suggested answers has led us to reread original papers, some from a decade or two ago. We have been pleased with this exercise for it has been a pleasure to find again the intellectual strength and adventure that the field of second language acquisition provides.

RESEARCH METHODOLOGY

Within the field of second language acquisition, there are many ways of eliciting and analyzing data. This section considers some of the predominant ways of collecting data and asks students to examine the type of information that is available depending on the way data are elicited.

When considering how second language data are collected, one must ask the question: Why would a researcher select one type of data collection procedure over another? What is most important in understanding the choice is an understanding of the relationship between a research question and research methodology. Although these may not always be in a 1:1 relationship, there are certain kinds of questions and certain kinds of external pressures that would lead one to select one type of research approach over another. If, for example, one wanted to gather information about how nonnative speakers learn to apologize in a second language, one could observe learners over a period of time, noting instances of apologizing (either in a controlled experiment or in a naturalistic setting). On the other hand, one could use a cross-sectional approach by setting up a situation and asking large groups of second language speakers at different proficiency levels what they would say in a particular situation. The latter forces production, the former waits until it happens. Although many would argue that the former is "better" in that it more accurately reflects reality, it is also clear that one might wait for a considerable amount of time before getting any information that would be useful in answering the original research question. Thus, the exigencies of the situation lead a researcher to a particular approach.

There are particular research frameworks that have typically relied on particular elicitation procedures. For example, research with theoretical linguistic underpinnings often uses acceptability judgments as a way of gathering data (see Problem 1.1); research on speech acts often uses discourse completion tasks as a tool for data elicitation. But even within these general categories there are methodological questions that need to be addressed. Taking acceptability judgments as a case in point, how are they to be done? Should they be timed? Should they be untimed? Should learners correct what they perceive to be an error or is that unnecessary? Should the sentences be contextualized or is it appropriate to consider isolated sentences? In this section and throughout the book research methodology should be questioned and analyzed. Students should be encouraged to consider to what extent the data may be an artifact of the elicitation procedure and, if so, what might be done differently to avoid a procedural bias.

Problem 1.1

Purpose: To reflect on the role of methodology in SLA research.
Data Source: Original and unpublished data.

Answers for this problem will depend on students' actual responses. The suggested answers are based on our experiences with students doing this problem.

In Part 4, the instructor polls all students for their collective responses. These responses are based on Part I. For example, for a class of 15 students, the responses might look like the following:

		1	2
1.	We didn't dare answer him back.	13	2
	We dared not answer him back.	2	13
2.	We didn't dare to answer him back.	6	9
	We didn't dare answer him back.	9	6
3.	We didn't dare to answer him back.	11	4
	We dared not answer him back.	4	11

Question 1
The responses will probably show that acceptability judgments are relative. That is, the responses as to the acceptability of each sentence will differ depending on what it is being compared to. Given the hypothetical scores from above, the responses to Sentence 1 would look like:

We didn't dare answer him back. (Group 1)	13	2
We didn't dare answer him back. (Group 2)	9	6

We dared not answer him back. (Group 1)	2	13
We dared not answer him back. (Group 3)	4	11

We didn't dare to answer him back. (Group 2)	6	9
We didn't dare to answer him back. (Group 3)	11	4

Question 2
The method is valid if what you are seeking is comparative judgments.

Question 3
For this question, students should use the Worksheets. Worksheet for Rating (p. 6) is to be used for Part Two. Worksheet for Ranking (p. 7) is to be used for Part Three. The numbers on the left for the Rating Worksheet represent the order these sentences appeared on the tape.

Students can work in groups. The worksheet format allows for up to 5 in a group. Each student should provide his/her score for each item. These scores are then summed, the mean can be provided (optional) and rank orders within each item are determined.
a. It will probably be found that different methods yield different results.
b. To obtain this information and if this part of the problem is assigned to be completed outside of class, ½ of the class can be asked to do it as a two choice response and the other half as a three choice response. Results can then be compared.
c. Advantage to rating: It is easier to give responses to single sentences.
     Disadvantage: Listening skills are involved in addition to purely judgment data. However, this could be given as a paper and pencil task without the complication of listening.

     Advantage to ranking: Listening is not involved (however, see above).
     Disadvantage: Comparing sentences to give relative rankings is not a task that one is generally called upon to do with language. Thus, in addition to actual judgments is the cognitive burden of sentence comparison.

<u>Additional Discussion</u>
Discussion based on these data can include a class discussion about elicitation methodology in general and how the type of data elicited is dependent on the methodology used. A discussion of this can be found in Gass & Selinker (1994), Chapter Two.

Problem 1.2

Purpose: To consider 1) avoidance and 2) the role of different methodologies in analysizing second language data.
Data Source: Unpublished data, Gass (1979).

<u>Question 1</u>
1. SU/GEN; 2. SU/OCOMP; 3. SU/IO; 4. OBJ/IO; 5. SU/DO; 6. OBJ/OCOMP; 7. OBJ/DO; 8. OBJ/SU; 9. OBJ/GEN; 10. SU/SU

<u>Question 2</u>
Errors are in the following sentences:
Learner 1: 2, 3, 4, 5, 6, 7 (many are errors because participants started with the second sentence)
Learner 2: 1, 2, 3, 4, 5, 6, 7, 9, 10
Learner 3: 1, 2, 3, 4, 5, 6, 9, 10
Learner 4: 1, 2, 3, 4, 5, 6, 7, 10
Learner 5: 1, 2, 3, 4, 5, 6, 7, 10

<u>Question 3</u>
The student errors tend to move the targetted structure higher on the Accessibility Hierarchy. For example, consider Learner 1, who made errors in sentences 2-7. In sentence 2, the targetted structure is an OCOMP relative, yet the produced structure is a SU relative. In sentences 3 & 4, the error did not have to do with a different relative clause structure. In sentence 5, the targetted structure was a DO relative, yet the produced structure is a SU relative. In 6, the change was from an OCOMP to a DO and in 7 there was no change in relative clause type. For learner 2, there were the following changes: 2. OCOMP to SU; 3. IO to SU; 4. IO to IO; 5. DO to SU; 6. OCOMP to SU; 7. DO to SU; 9. GEN to SU; 10. SU to SU. For learner 3, there were the following changes: 1. GEN to no relative clause; 2. OCOMP to SU; 3. IO to no relative clause; 4. IO to IO; 5. DO to SU; 6. OCOMP to OCOMP; 9. Error in form; 10. Error in form. For learner 4, there were the following changes: 1. Error in form; 2. OCOMP to SU; 3. IO to SU; 4. Error in form; 5. DO to SU; 6. OCOMP to SU; 7. DO to SU; 10. SU to SU. For learner 5, there were the following changes: 1. Error in form. 2. OCOMP to SU; 3. No relative clause; 4. No relative clause; 5. No relative clause; 6. OCOMP to DO; 7. DO to SU; 10. SU to SU.

<u>Question 4</u>
From question 3, we can see that when there were changes in relative clauses, the changes for the most part resulted in structures higher on the hierarchy. One could claim that learners avoided the targetted structure in as much as they did not follow the instructions. Examples of "avoidance" strategies was to use different words (bigger to smaller); change grammatical structures (active to passive); start with the second sentence, not use a relative clause at all.

<u>Question 5</u>
1. SU/GEN; 2. SU/OCOMP; 3. SU/IO; 4. OBJ/SU; 5. SU/SU; 6. SU/DO; 7. OBJ/DO; 8. OBJ/GEN; 9. OBJ/OCOMP; 10. OBJ/IO

<u>Question 6</u>
The answers should be: 1. Good; 2. Good; 3. Good; 4. Not good; 5. Good; 6. Good; 7. Not good; 8. Not good; 9. Not good; 10. Not good. In general, there were far more errors in the sentence combining task than the acceptability judgment task. This may be due to the demands of the task (production versus reception/interpretation). On the sentence combining task, the most accurate relative clause type was SU relatives. On the judgment task, there is a much wider range of correct responses. Below is an analysis per subject (C=correct; I=Incorrect)

Learner 1	Learner 2	Learner 3	Learner 4	Learner 5
1. C	I	I	I	I
2. I	I	C	I	I

3.	C	I	I	I	I
4.	I	I	C	C	C
5.	C	C	I	C	I
6.	C	I	C	C	C
7.	C	I	I	C	C
8.	I	C	I	C	C
9.	I	C	I	C	C
10.	C	C	I	C	C

For Learner 1, the only consistently wrong relative clause type was OCOMP. DO was the only consistently correct pattern.

For Learner 2, the only consistently wrong relative clause type was DO. Nothing was consistently right, however.

For Learner 3, IO and GEN were consistently wrong. Nothing was consistently right.

For Learner 4, SU and DO were consistently correct. Nothing was consistently wrong.

For Learner 6, DO was the only consistently correct pattern. Nothing was consistently wrong.

Question 7

Learner	Sentence Combining	Acceptability Judgment
1	Consistently Correct= SU Consistently Incorrect=DO, IO, OCOMP	Consistenlty Correct=DO Consistently Incorrect=OCOMP
2	Consistenltly Correct=nothing Consistenlty Incorrect=SU,IO,GEN,OCOMP	Consistenlty Correct=nothing Consistently Incorrect=DO
3	Consistently Correct=nothing Consistently Incorrect=DO,IO,OCOMP	Consistenlty Correct=nothing Consistently Incorrect=IO, GEN
4	Consistently Correct=nothing Consistently Incorrect=DO,IO,OCOMP	Consistenlty Correct=SU, DO Consistently Incorrect=nothing
5	Consistently Correct=nothing Consistently Incorrect=DO,IO,OCOMP	Consistenlty Correct=DO Consistently Incorrect=nothing

As can be seen, there is little consistency across elicitation types.

Additional Discussion

Classroom discussion can center around exactly what is being asked when one is being asked to do these tasks. What are the demands placed on learners? A second area for discussion can focus on the GEN, which should have been incorrect more often given its place on the Accessibility Hierarchy. This is discussed in Gass (referenced below), but the gist of the argument is that the GEN is seen as a unit and that unit can occupy different positions on the Hierarchy. For example, the sentence *I saw the boy [whose girlfriend] left him* may have been interpreted as a SU relative clause with [whose girlfriend] serving as the subject of the verb *left*. On the other hand, a sentence such as *I loved the boy whose girlfriend I saw yesterday* [a sentence not witnessed in these data] would be interpreted as a DO relative. This would then account for why these structures, interpreted as SU and DO relative clauses, were higher than they would have been expected to be.

Problem 1.3

Purpose: To illustrate that what NNSs say in conversation does not always coincide with an appropriate interpretation. Primary data appear to show that the learner understood the message but secondary data, in this case retrospective data, brings this conclusion into question.

Data Source: Hawkins, B. (1985). Is an "appropriate response" always so appropriate? In S. Gass & C. Madden (Eds.). *Input in Second Language Acquisition*. Rowley, MA: Newbury House.

Question 1
The NNS speaker says *yes/no* and *Uh huh* and repeats words which on first reading appear appropriate.

Question 2
NS provides a model such as:
Say, "What's it for?" You ask me, "What's it for?'

NS provides comprehension check: You don't know the name?

NS provides hints, e.g.: What else do you eat it with?

NS repeats with gestures: Smooth (gestures)

NS does foreigner talk, e.g.: is it for eat?

NS encourages NNS to guess, e.g. No....close!

Question 3

REPETITION	FUNCTION
Noise (Excerpt 1-NNS)	Comprehension
Noise (Excerpt 1-NS)	Conversational solidarity
No	Conversational solidarity
Metal (Excerpt 2 - NS)	Comprehension
What this for? (Excerpt 2-NNS)	Conversational solidarity
Sharp? (Excerpt 3-NNS)	Conversational solidarity
/smu/ (Excerpt 4 - NNS)	Seeks clarification
Smooth with gestures (Excerpt 4 - NS)	Help facilitate NN comprehension
Close (Excerpt 5 - NNS)	Seeks clarification
The knife. (Excerpt 5 - NNS)	Comprehension

Question 4
In general, conclusions based solely on primary data are suspect and present an outsider's, not a participant's point of view. In this case, without looking at retrospective comments, at times, you would think comprehension occurred when it clearly did not. Misunderstandings can go both ways: comprehension when it does not occur and misunderstandings when there might have been comprehension but when the learner does not have the metalanguage to explain.

Question 5
At times nothing happens. Often there is repetition and sometimes an explicit bit of help is provided.

Question 6
With retrospective data, one can determine with greater accuracy the extent to which understandings and intentions were in synch. They sometimes show exactly where and how misunderstandings happen.

Additional Discussion
A topic to pursue is the value of secondary data of various types. The secondary data here are retrospective data which means data collected by participants only. First, there are several types of problems with this type of data, an obvious one being the memory of the participants as to what they were trying to say.

Another topic that can be raised concerns other types of secondary data, such as expert data. Secondary data give insight into research questions by helping to guide the analysis. One may want to pursue the epistemological question of whether, in and of themselves, they prove anything.

Interlanguage Knowledge

This section deals with the different types of knowledge (lexical, syntactic, semantic, and phonological) that adult learners develop in the process of acquiring a second language.

Ever since the Interlanguage Hypothesis was originally proposed (Selinker, 1972), one of the fundamental assumptions of second language acquisition research has been that at every stage of the acquisition process learners have an internalized grammar (an interlanguage) that consists of their knowledge of the second language acquired up to that stage. Interlanguage grammars are constructed and continuously changed by learners on the basis of both the input they receive and the cognitive mechanisms that govern language learning. The knowledge represented in the interlanguage grammar may be metalinguistic (i.e., knowledge *about* the language), which is typically acquired in a classroom setting, or tacit (knowledge *of* the language), which may be acquired spontaneously through exposure to the L2 and interaction: It is an open question whether and to what extent these types of knowledge are represented and accessed separately. Many aspects of interlanguage grammars often do not resemble either the L1 or the L2, but rather represent a learner's novel and original hypotheses, and may typically look like structures that can be found in other natural languages.

Interlanguage knowledge underlies a learner's production in the L2, but only as one of several factors (ranging from processing strategies to socio/pragmatic abilities) that affect language use. For this reason, there is seldom a complete match between what learners know and what they can do in the L2. This is why interlanguage knowledge may be studied independently of the learner's ability to use it in concrete situations. A productive branch of SLA research focuses on the characteristics of interlanguage grammars at different stages of the acquisition process, in an attempt to answer questions such as "to what extent does the learner's L1 affect his/her L2 knowledge?", "what are the universal developmental paths that all learners tend to go through?", "how close to native-like competence can adult learners go?" This type of research, which tends to concentrate on syntactic knowledge, often uses acceptability judgments as the main source of data, on the assumption that they may reflect interlanguage knowledge more closely than production data.

In this section we have included different types of problems, in an attempt to do justice to the diversity of aims and approaches that can be found in SLA research. The first part of the section deals with lexical knowledge, or the nature of the "mental lexicon" that learners develop for a second language. The most relevant (and yet unresolved) question concerns the interdependence of the L1 lexicon and the L2 lexicon: Are L1 and L2 lexical entries connected and what is the nature of the connection (phonological? semantic?)? Do the two lexicons gradually separate with increasing proficiency? Are L2 learners inclined to rely on the L1 for all of the possible meanings of a word?

The second part of this section includes problems on syntactic knowledge. Some of these problems exemplify a type of SLA research that is explicitly related to contemporary linguistic theories on generative grammar, and focus on the acquisition of abstract syntactic principles such as, for example, Subjacency or Binding. Other problems focus on less abstract properties, such as auxiliaries, tense and aspect, and concentrate on the relative importance of syntax and semantics in language development.

Much of the data in this section are primarily obtained by means of acceptability judgment tasks (using a variety of methods) or other kinds of form-focused tasks (question-formation, word-manipulation). The main question addressed by these problems is whether the same kind of universal constraints that operate in child language acquisition (Universal Grammar, in the terminology commonly used) also guide adult second language acquisition. A related question is whether learners who have reached a near-native stage of proficiency in the second language have internalized the same kind of knowledge as monolingual native speakers of that language.

We have tried to make the data in this section accessible to students and teachers without a specific background in linguistics. We believe that the data are interesting regardless of the theoretical framework from which they were originally derived, and we have therefore reduced or eliminated much theoretical detail that can be found in the original sources. A small number of problems, however, would benefit from some understanding of the theoretical notions involved and would be best approached under the guidance of an instructor familiar with those approaches.

The last part of this section includes problems that focus on phonological knowledge in interlanguage. Here, the questions addressed are of a somewhat different nature from those addressed with respect to syntactic knowledge. Both the research in this domain and our everyday experience suggest that many learners who are otherwise very advanced in terms of second language proficiency nevertheless retain a foreign accent. Why should the phonetic, phonological, and prosodic properties of the second language be difficult to acquire? As in the case of lexical and syntactic knowledge, there often is a mismatch between perception and production. Some of the problems focus on the direction of this mismatch: Is perception better than production, or is it the other way around? Other problems consider the difference between underlying phonological representations and phonetic realizations, and the extent to which underlying representations are influenced by the phonological and prosodic structure of the L1. The data are elicited with a variety of perception and production tasks, but also come from spontaneous production.

Although most of the problems in this section focus on the acquisition of English by speakers of a variety of language backgrounds (Arabic, Chinese, Danish, Dutch, French, Indonesian, Japanese, Korean, Norwegian, Spanish, Taiwanese), some are concerned with the acquisition of other languages (French, Italian) by speakers of English and of other languages.

Problem 2.1

Purpose: To demonstrate fossilization in instances where the target language appears to have frozen syntax (e.g., metaphors and aphorisms).

Data Source: Selinker, L. (continually updated webbed database), The Applied Linguistics WWW Virtual Library, http://alt.venus.co.uk/VL/AppLingBBK/VLDB.html, Data Archives Section, Empirical pedagogy/interlanguage databases: Interlanguage Metaphors/Aphorisms

Question 1
There is sometimes disagreement among native speakers as to these meanings, which can provide excellent and interesting class discussion. The following present a consensus of agreed meanings culled from classes over a ten year period in the U.S. and U.K.:

1. When in Rome, do as the Romans (do).; or:
One must accommodate oneself to local customs.

2. She regularly shoots herself in the foot.; or:
She regularly sabotages herself.

3. I woke up fresh as a daisy.; or:
I woke up alert.

4. He is going to talk your ear off tonight.; or:
...talk at you without cessation.

5. To the victor belong the spoils.; or:
After a conflict, one benefits from what was at stake.

6. Britain has a great stake in the world, the Dutch do not.; or:
Britain has great (political) interests in the world; the Dutch, on the other
hand, have/do not.

7. I will be on your case about this one.; or:
I will bother you and not leave you alone concerning this matter.

8. No man is an island.; or:
Noone can live in isolation.

9. That was a very good chance for us to turn the tables (on him/her/them).or:
...change potential defeat into victory.

10. You can't have your cake and eat it too.; or:
Two things that you want are incompatible.

11. Take the monkey off our backs.; or:
A great burden was removed.

12. he'll have egg on his face; or:
he will become very embarrassed.

13.... which came to mind...; or:
came to your attention.

14. He will need something to save face.; or:
to avoid humiliation.

15. We must give him/her/them the benefit of the doubt.; or:
...give them every opportunity to defend themselves.

16. ...,then so be it.; or:
...that is just the way it will have to be.

17. I'm putting myself in her shoes.; or:
...imagining I am in the same situation.

18. We all have bees in our bonnet.; or:
We all have obsessions.

19. We won't take it lying down.; or:
We will not surrender easily.

20. They keep on moving the goal posts on us.; or
They keep changing the rules on us.

Question 2
The non-native speaker modifications can be described as follows:
2.1. When you are in Rome, you must do what Romans do.
The Japanese speaker of English here uses the major content words of the phrase: Rome, do, filling in the meaning of *be in a place,* but produces the elements in a native speaker English grammatical canonical word order: subject-verb-object in each clause.

2.2. She regularly shoots herself in her foot.
The Indian speaker of English here also has the major content words right but uses the possessive pronoun to mark the possession of the foot, which native speakers of English tend to do in most contexts *She washed her hands* not like in many other languages, where the generic article is used as in **She washed the hands*.

2.3. I woke up fresh as daisy.
The KiKongo/Lingala speaker of English here by NOT producing the expected article before the word daisy, unanimously in native speaker informal tests destroys the idiomatic meaning of *being alert* and raises the semantics of the person named Daisy, unfortunately almost in every case, producing mirth.

It may be the case that a uniform explanation is not possible though some widespread features are noticeable, for example, a tendency to remember major content words but not the specific syntax, a tendency to use canonical word order (English subject-verb-object) when frozen syntax should be used; a tendency to have trouble in the article/pronoun system and in the related singular/plural system and a related tendency to gap.

Question 3
If this expected native speaker frozen syntax is violated, then non-nativeness is very quickly noticed, no matter what the so-called proficiency level is of the interlanguage speaker. Also, these deviances often cause mirth among native speakers where none is intended, since a literal, often humorous unintended meaning is accessed. Interestingly, while some native speakers use these with their frozen syntax quite frequently and rapidly to make a point in colloquial speech, there appears to be no perceptual problem for non-native speakers here, once the meaning is explained. The frequency of use issue as input is interesting in that some advanced non-native speakers claim not to have heard them even after they are spoken in the environment.

Examples: In 3, where the non-native speaker said *I woke up fresh as daisy* invokes in, at least native speakers, the name Daisy.

In 5, where the non-native speaker said: *To victor belong spoils.*, it also invoked a name Victor.

Sentence 6, *Britain has a lot of stakes in the world, the Dutch have not* is heard by NSs as: *the British have a huge amount of (beef)steak* reminding those in Britain of mad cow disease.

When the non-native Dutch speaker is quoted in 7. as saying *I will be on your cases about this one*, native speakers hear the literal meaning of packing case.

Question 4

It is clear that this is an area of fossilization and that non-native speakers have problems trying to use these in production in correct TL syntax.

Not only do NNSs appear to easily remember the major content words of the fixed phrase while having trouble with the exact frozen syntax, but they also sometimes produce a grammatical TL sentence that just happens not to be the one that native speakers use. Ungrammatical TL sentences occur often in the related article/pronoun/sg/pl systems (3, 5, 7, 10, 11, 12, 18, 20)

Sometimes other IL processes appear to intersect and reinforce what is going on here, for example, overgeneralization of infinitives. An explanation for the frozen syntax here might be the cognitive invoking of the multiple effects principle in forcing a fossilization (cf Selinker & Lakshmanan (1992). With aphorisms these processes can at times produce forms such as: 19. *We won't take it to lie down.*; and 20. *They keep on to move the goal posts on us.*

Question 5

This exercise can generate huge amounts of class discussion. Experience shows that most of these aphorisms and metaphors have some sort of translation/pragmatic equivalent in other languages, often with very different words, but importantly, with a frozen syntax in that language. Interestingly, sometimes the changes are minor and in the same semantic field, like the substitute of feet for shoes in 17 above.

Additional Discussion:

It has been observed that if the frozen target language syntax of the aphorism is violated, then non-nativeness is blatant and noticed. This is interestingly true for even the Dutch, whose English is supposed to be so 'perfect'. Also, when there are clear jokes (see 4 above), near native speakers do not seem to get them without explicit and often prolonged explanation.

Rent the Fred Aistaire/Ginger Rogers 1937 film TOP HAT; there is a character there called Bardini who speaks a humorous Italian-English. He says such things as: *Let's face the musicians* for the obvious NS *Let's face the music*, which is also cleverly, a play on a hit song. Have the class list the aphorisms and metaphors Bardini produces and discuss if they match or deviate from the above generalizations about what non-native speakers seem to do with such daily expressions. Conduct a discussion on the topic of whether Hollywood of the '30s got it right, and if you wish, go into sensitive politically correct issues and interlanguage production.

Also, since some native speakers pepper their talk with these sorts of expressions, often slightly wrong, this would be an excellent opportunity to have the class do field work and perform various tests to see what non-native speakers do in interactions, especially with native speakers and what repair one might have to undergo.

Problem 2.2

Purpose: To explore the traditional idea that learners will transfer everything from the native language into the language being learned.

Data Source: Kellerman, E. (1979). Transfer and non-transfer: Where we are now. *Studies in Second Language Acquisition, 2,* 37-57. And Kellerman, E. (1986). An eye for an eye: Crosslinguistic constraints on the development of the L2 lexicon. In E. Kellerman & M. Sharwood Smith (Eds.), *Cross-linguistic influence in second language acquisition.* New York: Pergamon.

Question 1

Ordering % in ( ):
6. (81), 3. (79), 11. (64), 14. (61), 5.(60), 2(51), 16. (47), 4. (35), 12. (34), 8. (33), 1.(28), 17.(25), 7. (22), 10. (17), 15.(17), 9.(11) and 13.(9).

Question 2

Given the meanings of the Dutch sentences, the differences are, on the one hand, those which might be considered the most usual, the most frequent *(He broke his leg.; She broke his heart.)* and those which the learners believe are unique to the native language *(Some workers have broken the strike.; His voice broke when he was 13.)*. The most usual and most frequent are called core meanings and are the most transferable.

Question 3

If there is a universality to transferability, then similar results should obtain with this measure, with learners accepting in the target language those sentences highest on the scale.

Part Two:
Question 4.

The number of meanings that come out of a class can be surprising, with native speakers of various languages producing idioms non-native speakers have not even conceived of. An interesting cultural discussion can come from here, as, for example, whether the Biblical *eye for an eye* appears in non-Christian cultures and what the pragmatic equivalent might be.

Question 5

To reflect the relative translatability of the possible meanings of the Dutch word *eye*, we first can eliminate human *eye* since as Kellerman states: 'it very nearly totally dominates every other sense.'

Then one can transpose this table into another table that shows relative ordering such as:

potato is more likely to be preferred over dice	**10**
dice " **potato**	**25**
potato is more likely to be preferred over peacock	**6**
peacock " **potato**	**29**
potato is more likely to be preferred over needle	**3**
needle " **potato**	**32**
potato is more likely to be preferred over electronic	**0**
electronic " **potato**	**35**
peacock is more likely to be preferred over potato	**29**
potato " **peacock**	**6**
peacock is more likely to be preferred over dice	**22**
dice " **peacock**	**13**
peacock is more likely to be preferred over needle	**14**
needle " **peacock**	**21**
peacock is more likely to be preferred over electronic	**11**
electronic " **peacock**	**24**

and so on

The first thing one notices with this sort of regrouping is that not every two pairs is equally distributed, some that work with *potato* being closer to the natural human *eye*, others like those that work with peacock having a more varied distribution. It seems that the relative ordering can thus be established by closeness to primary sense of human eye, for example, eye of a needle and electronic eye perhaps related to eye of a peacock as opposed to the non-eye (in Dutch) or a potato or dice.

Question 6

Yes, the results from Part Two are in fact consistent with the results from Part One for the reasons stated above: primary/core meaning are more frequently seen as translatable.

Question 7
The conclusion drawn here on the basis of these data concerning the acquisition of lexical meaning in an L2 should be considered as hypothesis, not as fact: viz, that primary/core meanings will be acquired first and that transferability (and not predictable individual transfer) exists from the native language into the interlanguage, that is, this is one way the interlanguage is 'permeable'.

Additional Discussion
Given that this problem deals with "perceived transferability", profitable time can be spent on how these data relate to what actually is transferred at a particular time by particular learners.

Additionally, the interaction between syntax and semantics can be raised. The sentence *The cup broke* is judged as less possible in translation than *He broke his leg*, even though they are both examples of core meanings. This is most likely the case because *the cup broke* involves a marked syntactic phenomenon (the intransitivaztion of *break* and the promotion of the object to subject position.

Finally, given how little replication there is in second language acquisition, student attempts to replicate this study with other pairs of languages (not only typologically similar ones but typologically distant ones as well) would be very useful.

Problem 2.3

Purpose: To compare word associations between native speakers and nonnative speakers.
Data Source: Meara, P. (1978). Learners' word associations in French, *Interlanguage Studies Bulletin, 3,* 192-211.

Question 1
The category : , the largest category with 40 responses, reflects words that are not the usual primary responses of native French speakers. (the category / has 37 responses and the category = has 23.

There were 23 responses under category marked =, indicating learner responses that are the same as French speaker responses. They are listed below:

#	Stimulus	Gloss	response	Gloss
1	table	table	chaise	chair
5	homme	man	femme	woman
8	manger	eat	boire	drink
9	montagne	mountain	neige	snow
11	noir	black	blanc	white
14	main	hand	pied	foot
15	petit	small	grand	large
16	fruit	fruit	pomme	apple
17	papillon	butterfly	fleur	flower
20	chaise	chair	table	table
23	femme	woman	homme	man
24	froid	cold	chaud	warm
26	désirer	desire	vouloir	want
28	blanc	white	noir	black
40	fille	girl	garçon	boy
46	soldat	soldier	guerre	war
49	aigle	eagle	oiseau	bird
57	garçon	boy	fille	girl
69	océan	ocean	mer	sea
73	religion	religion	église	church
78	soif	thirst	faim	hunger
96	rue	street	maison	house
97	roi	king	reine	queen

There were 40 responses under category marked :, indicating learner responses that are not the usual primary responses of native French speakers, but that do nevertheless occur in the list of their normal responses. They are listed below:

#	Stimulus	Gloss	NS response	Gloss	NNS response	Gloss
2	sombre	dark	clair	light	sun	soleil
10	maison	house	toit	roof	jardin	garden
12	agneau	lamb	doux	meek	mouton	sheep
25	lent	slow	rapide	quick	vite	fast
27	rivière	river	fleuve	large river	mer	sea
30	fenêtre	window	rideau	curtain	porte	door
33	pied	foot	chaussure	shoe	main	hand
36	rouge	red	noir	black	bleu	blue
41	haut	high	bas	low	montagne	mountain
44	terre	land/ earth	mer	sea	ciel	sky
45	difficulté	difficulty	facilité	facility	facile	easy
50	estomac	stomach	digestion	digestion	manger	eat
51	tige	stem	fleur	flower	tigre	tiger
53	rêve	dream	sommeil	(state of) sleep	dormir	to sleep
55	pain	bread	vin	wine	beurre	butter
58	clair	clear/light	obscur	dark	lune	moon
60	évangile	gospel	bible	bible	église	church
63	bain	bath/ swim(n.)	mer	sea	salle de bain	bathroom
64	villa	villa	mer	sea	maison	house
65	rapide	rapid	train	train	vite	quick
66	bleu	blue	mer	sea	rouge	red
67	faim	hunger	soif	thirst	manger	eat
70	tête	head	cheveux	hair	yeux	eyes
72	long	long	court	short	petit	small
74	cognac	brandy	alcool	alcohol	boire	drink
75	enfant	child	petit	small	bébé	baby
79	ville	city	paris	paris	maison	house
81	beurre	butter	jaune	yellow	pain	bread
82	docteur	doctor	maladie	illness	hôpital	hospital
84	voleur	thief	bicyclette	bicycle	cambrioleur	burglar
85	lion	lion	crinière	mane	tigre	tiger
87	lit	bed	repos	rest	dormir	sleep
89	tabac	tobacco	fumée	smoke	pipe	pipe
90	bébé	baby	rose	pink	enfant	child
91	lune	moon	nuit	night	clair	light
93	tranquille	quiet	calme	calm	silence	silence
94	vert	green	pré	meadow	bleu	blue
98	fromage	cheese	blanc	cream (cheese)	pain	bread
99	fleur	flower	rose	rose	jardin	garden
100	effrayer	frighten	peur	fear	enfant	child

There were 37 responses under category marked /, indicating learner responses that are not normally produced by native French speakers. They are listed below:

#	Stimulus	Gloss	NS response	Gloss	NNS response	Gloss
3	musique	music	note	note	disque	record
4	maladie	illness	lit	bed	malade	sick
6	profond	deep	puits	well	plafond	ceiling
7	mou	soft	dur	hard	vache	cow
13	confort	comfort	fauteuil	armchair	confortable	comfortable

18	lisse	smooth	rugueux	rough	livre	book
19	ordre	order	désordre	disorder	demander	ask
21	doux	sweet/ soft	dur	hard	deux	two
22	sifflet	whistle	train	train	soufflé	soufflé
29	beau	beautiful	joli	pretty	belle	beautiful
31	rugueux	rough	lisse	smooth	rouge	red
32	citoyen	citizen	vote	vote	auto	car
34	araignée	spider	toile	(cob) web	arranger	arrange
35	aiguille	needle	fil	thread	train	train
37	sommeil	sleep	lit	bed	soleil	sun
38	colère	anger	rouge	red	bleu	blue
39	tapis	carpet	moëlleux	soft	eau	water
42	travail	work	repos	rest	école	school
43	aigre	sour	doux	sweet	tigre	tigeer
47	chou	cabbage	(chou) fleur	cauliflower	chat	cat
48	dur	hard	mou	soft	sur	on
52	lampe	lamp	lumière	light	lit	bed
54	jaune	yellow	vert	green	vieux	old
56	justice	justice	balance	balance	police	police
59	santé	health	maladie	illness	noël	Christmas
61	mémoire	memory	souvenir	remember	tête	head
62	mouton	sheep	doux	soft	vache	cow
68	prêtre	priest	noir	black	prendre	take
71	fourneau	oven	cuisine	kitchen	*tourneau	*(no meaning)
76	amer	bitter	doux	sweet	aimer	like
77	marteau	hammer	pilon	pestle	manteau	coat
80	carré	square	rond	round	voiture	car
83	bruyant	noisy	enfant	child	brille	shine
86	joie	joy	tristesse	sadness	joli	pretty
88	lourd	heavy	léger	light	silence	silence
92	ciseaux	scissors	couper	cut	cheveux	hair
95	sel	salt	mer	sea	acheter	buy

The largest category is the category marked :, indicating learner responses that are not the usual primary responses of native French speakers, but that do nevertheless occur in the list of their normal responses. 40 responses can be found in this category. Category marked : is closely followed by category marked /, indicating learner responses that are not normally produced by native French speakers with 37 responses.

Question 2
Apparently, common words evoke native-like responses of a 'paradigmatic' type (see Meara below) for example, table/chair, man/woman. Words which are less frequent evoke either paradigmatic responses *maladie/lit/malade* (illness/bed/sick), or involve esponses which are based on sound e.g. deep-*profond*/well-*puits*/ceiling-*plafond*.

Examples of paradigmatic responses

#	Stimulus	Gloss	NS response	Gloss	NNS response	Gloss
3	musique	music	note	note	Disque	record
4	maladie	illness	lit	bed	Malade	sick

Examples of syntagmatic responses

#	Stimulus	Gloss	NS response	Gloss	NNS response	Gloss
12	agneau	lamb	doux	meek	Mouton	sheep

Native French speakers make an association with the expression 'doux comme un agneau' (soft as a lamb), Non-native speakers do not.

| 36 | rouge | red | noir | black | bleu | blue |

Native French speakers make an association with the book by Stendhal *Le rouge et le noir* (Black and red), Non-native speakers do not.

Question 3
Associations in the category marked / rely mainly on form. Interestingly, less frequent words produce what Meara calls 'clang associates', non-French associations that are based on orthographical or phonological form, for example, *profond/puits/plafond* (deep/well/ceiling) and *doux/dur/deux* (soft/hard/two).

Examples of orthographical responses:

| 76 | amer | bitter | doux | sweet | Aimer | like |
| 86 | joie | joy | tristesse | sadness | Joli | pretty |

Where *amer* looks like *aimer* and *joli'* looks like *joie*

| 6 | profond | deep | puits | well | plafond | ceiling |
| 95 | sel | salt | mer | sea | acheter | buy |

Where *profond* sounds like 'plafond' and *sel* sounds like 'sell', the opposite of 'buy'.

Question 4
There seems to be a misunderstanding based on the interpretation of the French stimulus as a French or an English word form. French word forms: *citoyen* (#32 citizen) interpreted as Citroen with the response auto (car), *jaune* (#54 yellow) interpreted as *jeune*, meaning young, with the response *vieux* (old). English word forms: *mou* (#7 soft) interpreted as 'moo', a sound made by a *vache* (cow); *sel* (#95 salt) interpreted as sell, associated with the response *acheter* (buy).

Question 5
Learners rely heavily on phrases from L1, for example *bread and butter* and practical functions, for example *stomach/eat*, or concrete objects, for example instead of saying *souvenir* in response to *memory* they say *head*.

Question 6
23 cases out of 100. (Meara points out that these are basically 'translation equivalents' of the native form).

Question 7
Meara found that the learners' mental lexicon seems to lack 'proper semantic organization' in that, to paraphrase, lexical knowledge is sometimes tied to cross-linguistic phonetic associations. On the other hand, Healey (1998) has results which suggest that the mental lexicon of bilinguals is organized on semantic lines.

Additional Discussion
One area of discussion is the test itself. The word association test was adapted from psychoanalysis; it measured responses between certain types of patients and so-called 'normal' adults. A topic for discussion can be the extent to which it is appropriate to use such a test to compare native speakers and second language learners. Meara provides extensive justification for the adapted use which can be brought into the discussion.

Another area for discussion is the area of reliability and validity. What do these free associations, even if reliable, tell us about how the semantics of a language or an interlanguage as organized for productive and receptive use of language? Also, what could these percentages be hiding in terms of individual differences?

Finally, students could consider work by Healey (available on the web at http://lang80.lang.bbk.ac.uk/healey.htm) which extends Meara's word associations to a new population. Healey attempted to discover what types of French word associations were produced by non-native speakers of French versus native French speakers, both groups living and working in an English speaking environment. She found that primary responses from both groups paradoxically shared both commonality and diversity: that is, there were more native-like responses from non-native speakers than Meara found. All responses were more diverse, showing a variety of paradigmatic and syntagmatic associations. And, importantly, there were no clang associates. Study the detail of her results there and compare them to the results obtained by Meara.

Problem 3.1

Purpose: 1) To show that "what you see" is not always "what you get". That is, surface forms may not accurately reflect underlying grammars; 2) to show the importance of prefabricated patterns; and 3) to show gradual progression in acquisition.

Data Source: Hakuta, K. (1974). Prefabricated patterns and the emergence of structure in second language learning. *Language Learning, 24,* 287-297. (Part One); Ravem, R. (1968). *International Review of Applied Linguistics, 6,* 165-185. (Reprinted in *Error Analysis,* J. Richards (Ed.) (1974). London: Longman.

Question 1
At Month 1 the child seems to know the target grammar of English or at least has a close approximation. One important generalization involves the proper use of do-support and inversion.

Question 2
At Month 2, the child does not use the same generalizations as at Month 1 though *do you* is carried over. At this point, new interlanguage-particular forms (*What do you doing...*) appear. At month 2 a new form, the progressive, appears and the phrase *do you* appears in each question (Hakuta calls these *prefabricated patterns/routines*; others label them *chunks.*). *Do you* thus appears to be a question marker only and is not being analysed into its component parts *do + you.* Evidence for the lack of analysis of *do you* comes from the fact that *do you* is being used even when a third person singular subject occurs. From the data at Time 2, one can return to the data at Time 1. It is likely that the *doyou* at Month 1 was probably unanalysed and was only coincidentally correct. It is perhaps noteworthy that Japanese has a question marker *ka*, placed at the end of a sentence. Perhaps the existence of a question marker in this child's first language led her to "search the input" for a comparable form. This she found in questions addressed to her "Do you like this? Or Do you want this?".

Question 3
Looking at this child's use of *wh-* words, one sees that they are all used in sentence-initial position in the interlanguage, what one might not expect given the linguistic information about Japanese above, i.e. the word order of Japanese does not transfer here. One may see evidence of stages in that *why-* questions do not appear in bulk until month 10. The use of the other *wh-* words also seem to cluster and it may be that the child does not use a new *wh-*word until a previous one is mastered, which also argues for stages that may be abrupt.

Question 4
Past tense questions during Months 6-8 seem to relate to most instances of the *wh-* word *what.* This may be an accident of sampling. *Do you* still seems to function as a chunk with past tense irregular forms, though the tense with *put* may be also ambiguous in the interlanguage. The use of *did* enters more but may be a prefabricated pattern *did X V* varying target and non-target like structures: *Did you call?; cf.: Did everybody saw....?*

Question 5
In general, this child seems to follow stages from apparently perfect TL-like questions to more idiosyncratic interlanguage forms when new functions are introduced. Also, this child may very well need to master a form before trying out new ones, as stated above.

Question 6
Class discussion could be varied here; one thing is that one would like to see a much larger data base to see if sampling presented is typical of the whole or idiosyncratic.

Question 7
Apparently at Time 1, the child in *wh-* questions is mostly using a declarative sentence word order: *you reading; she (is) doing...,* and not inversion as in the NL. However, inversion seems

to happen in *yes/no* questions early on and carries into Time 2, *Climb you?*, and Time 3: *Like you ice cream?*, and beyond. Do-support seems to come in early and is manifest in Time 2: *What d'you like?*, but repetition task deletes it, perhaps showing it is unstable, even though Norwegian appears to have a similar construction. Time 4 presents mostly perfect target language- like constructions, though limited to negative questions.

Question *8
Even at the earliest stages neither child seems to be using a direct language transfer strategy with wh-questions, i.e. that is, we do not see in the Japanese-English interlanguage, questions such as: *That, what is?; You, how like?...*; or in Norwegian-English: *What reading you?; What doing she now?...* That is, this occurs even in languages as close as English and Norwegian. However, in this child's English yes/no questions, inversion as in the NL seems to happen early on. Time 3 shows a much greater use of *do* with a large variety of structures, including some interesting constructions such as: *What d'you did to-yesterday?* For this latter, Ravem's explanation is revealing here:
> It is as if (the child) ... is searching for a morpheme to attach tense to.

Question *9
With the child in Part One, one sees evidence of discontinuity in that one *wh-* word does not appear until late, though this may be an accident of sampling or individual personality, as some kids are always asking why. The use of other *wh-* words seem to cluster discretely with the suggestion that the child does not use a new *wh-* word until a previous one is mastered, which would be a strong argument for discontinuity. The *do* support data, however, appears throughout. One can note what is called U-shaped behavior in that the earliest sample appears to provide more target-like behavior than a later one with the target-like behavior then reappearing at the most advanced states.

With the child in Part Two, there seems to be an important stage where *do* as a support verb enters the interlanguage massively (but maybe not carrying tense as appears to be the case in TL English) and is tried in all sorts of constructions.

Additional Discussion:
An obvious topic is the role of *prefabricated routines* or *chunks* in second language acquisition; see the above two sources and the various textbooks (passim) for more updated discussion.

One important topic that always seems to arise involves the differences between various types of second language acquisition: child monolingual vs. adult; child monolingual vs. child bilingual; child bilingual vs. adult. There is no unified discussion in the literature pulling all of these together and disciplined speculation has to be taught. Ravem claims that
> The situation of the learner of a second language is clearly different from that of the L1 child. The most obvious difference is that the task of the foreign learner is not to learn LANGUAGE, which he already possesses and the knowledge of which must affect his acquisition of a second language.

A related issue is the area of stages in second language learning. Are there developmental stages? Can they be altered through instruction?

Problem 3.2

Purpose: To understand 1) the existence of stages in the naturalistic acquisition of L2 syntax, and to determine the extent to which they are affected by the L1, 2) the use of prefabricated patterns in early second language acquisition, 3) the phenomenon of 'fossilization', 4) the importance of affective variables and 'acculturation', and 5) the importance of different types of input (i.e., native versus non-native).

Data source: Schumann, J. 1978. *The Pidginization Process: A Model for Second Language Acquisition*. Rowley, MA: Newbury House.

Question 1
In the early stages this learner seem to produce correct English utterances. Examination of subsequent production, however, suggests that early utterances must be unanalysed 'routines'. Week 2 is characterized by the use of the negator in preverbal position, without an overt subject. In Week 7, the negator appears between the subject and the verb; the learner begins to use the

form *don't* in the same position as *no*. The forms 'don't and *no* continue to have the same distribution throughout the data sample: this shows that *don't* is not analysed as the contracted form of *do + not*, but is used as an alternative realization of *no*. The learner does not seem to progress from unanalysed *don't* to analysed and productive use of *do + not*. Evidence of progress would be, for example, the appearance of forms of *do* agreeing with the third person singular subject, as in *he doesn't*, but there is no such evidence in the data available. The learner seems to have stopped progressing towards the target: he has 'fossilized'.

Question 2
The few examples of modal verbs used by the learner consist of *can* (Weeks 7, 11, 21, 27, 35), and *will* (Week 11). These verbs are negated in the same way as all other verbs, i.e. by *don't* or *no* in pre-verbal position. The learner never acquires knowledge of the difference between main verbs and auxiliary verbs in English, that is, the fact that main verbs require the support of *do* whereas the latter do not.

Question 3
Descriptively, the acquisition of English negation entails four stages: 1) negator *no* in preverbal position, 2) negators *no* and *don't* in preverbal position, 3) appearance of copulas, auxiliaries and modals with negator in post-verbal position, and 4) target use of do-support (analysed *don't*) with main verbs only.

This learner does not seem to progress beyond the second stage.

Question 4
The data in Part Two are different from those in Part 1 because they are not spontaneous utterances. Following a short period of explicit instruction on negation, the learner was given sentences in declarative form and was asked to turn them into negative sentences. This task involves the application of metalinguistic knowledge in a de-contextualized situation. The data are consistent with those in Part 1: the learner's responses are based on the same interlanguage grammar, in which *don't* and *no/not* freely alternate in pre-verbal position. Explicit instruction does not seem to have altered the learner's interlanguage grammar.

Additional Discussion
In relation to question 2, for students with some knowledge of syntax: English thematic verbs do not raise past the negator, but English auxiliary verbs do. English is different from other languages in this respect: French, for example, has verb raising with both thematic and auxiliary verbs.

Problem 3.3

Purpose:	To focus on 1) parametric variation related to 'Verb Raising' in generative grammar and its implications for language acquisition, 2) the effects of parameter setting on a cluster of properties; short-term and long-term effects of 'negative evidence' (metalinguistic explanation, error correction), and 3) interaction between different types of knowledge (i.e., 'tacit' vs 'explicit') in the development of interlanguage grammars.
Data Source:	White, L. (1991). Adverb placement in second language acquisition: some effects of positive and negative evidence in the classroom. *Second Language Research* 7. 133-161.

Question 1
In the pretest all Francophone learners accept and produce sentences exemplifying the SVAO pattern, such as *Mary speaks very well English*, which is ungrammatical in English.

Question 2
In the first post-test, the patterns of responses given by the Adverb group and the Question group diverge: the Adverb group, who have been presented with explicit negative evidence about adverb placement in English, reject SVAO sentences; the Question group, who have received explicit instruction about question formation but not adverb placement, still accept SVAO as possible in English.

Question 3

The differences between the two experimental groups is clearly related to the different focus of the instruction they had received. Only the group explicitly instructed on adverb placement has learned that no adverbs can be placed between the verb and the direct object. The group explicitly instructed on question formation, on the other hand, has not learned knowledge of adverb placement (presumably they have learned knowledge about question formation but this was not tested).

Question 4

Explicit instruction seems to be beneficial in the short term: in the post-test given immediately after exposure to instruction, learners show a clear improvement with respect to their performance in the pretest.

Question 5

Explicit knowledge of question formation clearly does not generalize to knowledge of adverb placement, even though both these properties are assumed to derive from the same parameter setting (+Verb Raising for French, -Verb Raising for English). One can speculate why this is so. One possibility is that properties associated with the same parameter would cluster only in naturalistic, but not in instructed, acquisition. Another possibility is that the time interval between the explicit instruction period and the post-test was too short for any generalizing effects to take place. The third possibility is that the properties are not related after all: crucial evidence that would decide on this issue is that from first language acquisition, since the presence of clustering in child grammars would be powerful evidence in favor of the theory. It would be interesting to discuss what constitutes evidence of clustering in child and adult language acquisition: if one of the criteria is 'simultaneous appearance of the different properties at the same stage of development', how could this be determined?

Question 6

The fact that the Adverb group revert to their pretest performance a year after the experiment suggests that the knowledge acquired as a result of explicit instruction does not last. Perhaps this knowledge is only a short-term effect of the instruction and does not cause any deep changes in the learners' interlanguage grammar.

Question 7

It is possible that learners do not get much positive evidence of adverb placement in naturalistic input, so that even if learners continued to study English and perhaps were exposed to naturalistic input, this evidence would not be frequent and/or 'robust' enough to be 'noticed'. One can speculate whether these learners received any further explicit instruction on adverb placement in the classroom (and whether this is in fact a feature of instructional syllabi in different learning environments).

Question 8

Based on the results of this study, one might conclude that explicit instruction has short-lived or superficial effects, i.e. it does not 'engage UG'.

Additional Discussion

Evidence in support of the conclusion from Question 8 (given in the original source but not in the data available here) is the fact that explicit instruction on adverb placement leads learners to reject sentences of the form SVAX, which are perfectly grammatical in English. In these sentences, the verb is intransitive and the adverb is followed by a constituent other than a direct object, for example, by a prepositional phrase, such as *Mary walks quickly to school*. Learners who come to reject these sentences have learned an over-general, conscious rule that prohibits the placement of adverbs between the verb and any constituent.

Problem 3.4

Purpose:	To focus on 1) ultimate attainment in second language acquisition, 2) UG constraints and parametric variation, and 3) L1 influence.
Data Source:	Schachter, J. Testing a proposed universal. In S. Gass and J. Schachter (Eds.). *Linguistic Perspectives on Second Language Acquisition* (pp. 73-88). Cambridge: Cambridge University Press.

Question 1
The majority of native speakers pass both the syntax and the subjacency tests (although not for all the sentence types). The non-native subjects, however, perform differently. Although most of them can recognize the structures (as shown by the total numbers of subjects falling into cells A and C), only a few fall into cell A, that is, have knowledge of both syntax and subjacency constraints. A substantial number of non-native subjects fall into cell C: they pass the syntax test but fail the subjacency test.

Question 2
The pattern of native responses supports Hypothesis 1.

Question 3
The pattern of non-native responses does not support either Hypothesis 1 or Hypothesis 2. The most common response type for the non-natives is that characterized by cell C: knowledge of a syntactic construction without knowledge of subjacency constraints.

Question 4
Of the three non-native groups, the Korean speakers have more responses in cell C than the Indonesian and the Chinese subjects. This is probably related to the fact that Korean does not have subjacency, whereas Indonesian and Chinese show limited evidence of subjacency. Success in the acquisition of English subjacency seems therefore to be related to whether and to what extent the learners' native language instantiates this constraint. The Koreans do not show evidence of having acquired the constraint, even though they have acquired the construction in question. The Indonesian and Chinese learners have somewhat more of an advantage, but they fail to reach a native level of knowledge of subjacency constraints. The existence of subjacency in their native language does not seem to facilitate the extension of such knowledge to new contexts.

Question 5
Recall that the hypotheses were that (a) subjects who pass the syntax test also pass the subjacency test (therefore falling into cell A), and (b) subjects who fail the syntax test also fail the subjacency test (therefore falling into cell D). By combining cells A and D, we have an idea of how many subjects within each group perform as predicted. As for relative clauses, 10 out of 20 Indonesian learners, 14 out of 20 Chinese learners, and 13 out of 21 Korean learners behave as predicted. As for noun complements, 9 out of 20 Indonesians, 11 out of 20 Chinese, and 6 out of 21 Koreans behave as predicted. As for embedded questions, 13 out of 20 Indonesians, 9 out of 20 Chinese, and 8 out of 21 Koreans behave as predicted. By looking at the number of subjects in cell C we have an idea of how many subjects have knowledge of a syntactic construction but not of subjacency constraints: For relative clauses, 9 Indonesians, 6 Chinese, and 8 Koreans; For noun complements, 11 Indonesians, 9 Chinese and 15 Koreans; For embedded questions, 6 Indonesians, 9 Chinese and 13 Koreans.

Question 6
There does not seem to be any noticeable difference among the three sentence types represented in the table in terms of relative difficulty, except perhaps for noun complements for which a slightly greater number of learners within each group appear to have syntactic knowledge but not knowledge of subjacency violations. The data in the table confirm that the Koreans are the group with the least knowledge of subjacency constraints, as shown by the number of Korean learners who fall into cell C for the three sentence types.

Question 7
These findings suggest that Universal Grammar may not be operative in second language acquisition. If it were, there would be no barriers to the acquisition of constraints such as subjacency, regardless of the facts of the native language.

Problem 3.5

Purpose: To consider the following questions: What do near native speakers know of the target language that is fundamentally different from the vast majority of interlanguage speakers? Is the quality of linguistic information that such speakers know the same or different as native speakers? Are their competences the same? And, finally, can NNSs ever become NSs?

Data Source: Coppieters, R. (1987). Competence differences between native and non-native speakers. *Language, 63,* 544-573.

Question 1
One can immediately see a divergence in the charts. As seen in Figure 1, near-native speakers varied from the prototypical norm with a range from about 23% to about 49% of the sentences, whereas, native speakers varied on these same sentences from between below 5% to about 16% at the highest. These are quantitative results and do not prove that on a qualitative structural level there are important native/near native differences; for this we have to go structure by structure:

Question 2

The NS order is:	Native
Articles (8)	15%
Obj. + Pred. (28)	14.3%
Place of the Adj. (14)	11.8%
Il/elle vs. ce (10)	10.0%
a/de + Infinitive (2)	6.0%
de + Adj. (10)	6.0%
Imperf. vs. Pres. Perf. (5)	2.0%

The Near Native order is:	Near-Native
Imperf. vs. Pres. Perf. (5)	41.5%
a/de + Infinitive (2)	40.7%
Place of the Adj. (14)	38.1%
Il/elle vs. ce (10)	35.7%
Articles (8)	34.9%
Obj. + Pred. (28)	33.2%
de + Adj. (10)	22.9%

The reasons for the differences appear to be speculative and based on commonsense, but far from definitive. Take *Il/elle* vs. *ce*; they are both in the same place in the hierarchy, with NS intuitions fairly stable at 10%, while the NNS are more variable at almost 36. Clearly both have developed a grammar that distinguishes, but maybe not on grammatical grounds: Coppieters reports on qualitative comments that are mostly pragmatic, such as what sounds more natural and what they imply. The total flip-flop of Imperf. vs. Pres. Perf. is interesting with NS's having

...a strong and marked contrast between the imparfait and the passe compose... (p. 559)
Prepositions are hard for NNSs and would be expected to be at the top of the list, but why adjectives are is not clear.

Another measure can be gained by subtracting the raw % deviation of NS from the consistently larger NNS; thus:

	Native	Near-Native	Difference
Il/elle vs. ce (10)	10.0%	35.7%	= 25.7%
Place of the Adj. (14)	11.8%	38.1%	= 26.3%
Imperf. vs. Pres. Perf. (5)	2.0%	41.5%	= 39.5%
a/de + Infinitive (2)	6.0%	40.7%	= 34.7%
de + Adj. (10)	6.0%	22.9%	= 16.9%
Obj. + Pred. (28)	14.3%	33.2%	= 18.9%
Articles (8)	15%	34.9%	= 19.9%

Therefore the ordering is:	
Imperf. vs. Pres. Perf. (5)	39.5%
a/de + Infinitive (2)	34.7%
Place of the Adj.	26.3%
Il/elle vs. ce	25.7%
Articles (8)	19.9%
Obj. + Pred. (28)	18.9%
de + Adj. (10)	16.9%

These results perhaps back up the reality, though hard to explain, of these degrees of deviations. It is always interesting to ask the class exactly what they think these are measures of and whether the fact that the different number of sentences in each grammatical grouping could potentially vitiate the results.

Question 3
Given that the two foci are intertwined, this question can be creatively answered by either first going by language background, or instead, starting with each grammatical construction, which is what we choose to do here, and then summarizing by language group.

Il/elle vs. ce: The greatest divergence is with Farsi speakers, but of course there are only two and this imbalance should be noted. The other groups did more or less equally.

Il/e Obj. + Pred. : Again we have one group that did differently from the others, in this case, Germanic.

de + Adj. : Again, Germanic does worse than the others.

a/de + infinitive: This time both Japanese/Korean and Germanic show greater difference.

Imperf. vs. Pres. Perf.:   Here there may be a clear result with Romance showing the least difference, perhaps because these languages are the only ones to mirror French in having this grammatical distinction.

Place of the Adj.: Here there is a progression, with Farsi showing the greatest difference.

Articles: Here the differences seem to be greatest with Farsi and Japanese/Korean showing the greatest difference, which may relate, at least in the latter to the distinction having/not having articles. But why Romance and Germanic should show such a deviance cannot be due to NL structure. Thus, NL sometimes seems to play a role in the interpretation of the structures outlined above, most particularly in the imperfect/past contrast.

Note that in general, in this study, there seems no principled way to determine when NL transfer occurs and when it is blocked.

Question 4
This question seems to get good discussion from Japanese/Korean students, often wondering why these data were pooled by Coppieters.

Question 5
This question too will often produce quite a lot of discussion, the trick being to raise the students' form of discussion from anecdotes to careful hypotheses. A useful thing to do here is to have the students cite one or two definitions from the literature for class discussion.

Question *6
This study has been a source of debate and puzzlement since it first appeared in 1987. What exactly was Coppieters able to measure? The significance of the problem has never been in doubt: can non-native speakers ever become native speakers and is there a critical period beyond which native-speakerhood becomes impossible? The answers are hard to judge unambiguously. For example, there are clearly some very famous writers who write even better than most native speakers. In English one could think of Joseph Conrad (NL: Polish) or in French, Samuel Beckett (NL: English). And there are eloquent non-native speakers (e.g., Henry Kissinger whose NL is German). But, if you hear interviews with them, they are clearly non-native speakers (interestingly, some tapes still exist of Conrad speaking Polish- English in the early part of the century).

Additional Discussion:
Concerning language transfer, one could discuss whether transfer occurs only in interlanguage production vs. perceptual judgements as here.

One could take some of the authors mentioned in (6) and look at their writing (e.g., *Darkness at Noon* always leads to good discussion.) and discuss in the above terms. You could try to get an audio tape of these in an interview situation, especially Joseph Conrad. When these tapes are listened to, the non-native quality of their interlanguage talk becomes clear and not debatable. You could have students compare some features of their oral interlanguage with their written (is it still interlanguage?).

Finally, the class may wish to compare with a replication by Birdsong (1992).

Problem 3.6

Purpose: To consider 1) the question of 'ultimate attainment': the grammatical knowledge attained by near-native speakers, i.e., learners who have reached the highest level of L2 competence, 2) whether near-native knowledge is identical to the native knowledge of monolingual speakers, 3) whether there is evidence of L1 influence at the near-native level, and 4) optionality in the input and whether learners acquire it.

Data Source: Sorace, A. (1993). Incomplete vs divergent representations of unaccusativity in near-native grammars of Italian. *Second Language Research 9*, 22-48.

Question 1

Figure 1 ("Optional auxiliary change") shows that French near-native speakers of Italian accept only the sentence with the auxiliary *avere* and reject the sentence with the auxiliary *essere*, even though both are grammatical in Italian (as shown by the judgments of the native Italians). English near-native speakers, on the other hand, neither decisively accept nor decisively reject either of the two sentences: their judgments are indeterminate, i.e. they do not show a clear preference for one or the other, or a clear acceptance or rejection of both. Figure 2 ("Obligatory auxiliary change with clitic movement"), shows that the judgments of the French near-natives are similar to the judgments of native Italians: both groups correctly accept the sentence with *essere* and reject the one with *avere*. The English near-natives are again indecisive: they do not have a clear preference for either sentence and their judgments are indeterminate, as shown by the fact that the acceptability scores for both sentences are in the middle of the range. Figure 3 ("No movement - optional auxiliary change") displays a similar pattern to that of Figure 1: the French subjects accept the sentence with *avere* and tend to reject the one with *essere*, despite the fact that they are both acceptable in Italian; the English subjects do not have a clear preference, nor do they clearly accept or reject both sentences. The overall conclusion is that the near-native knowledge of the French subjects is convergent with respect to clitic movement, but divergent with respect to optional auxiliary change: their judgments are determinate but systematically different from the judgments of native speakers. The near-native knowledge of English subjects is incomplete with respect to all the syntactic phenomena in question: their judgments are indeterminate across the board.

Question 2

French, like Italian, has a choice of auxiliaries, but not in the construction exemplified by these sentences, where only the auxiliary *avoir* can be used. The French equivalent of both *Mario è dovuto andare a casa* and *Mario ha dovuto andare a casa* is *Mario a du aller à la maison*. Similarly, for both *Mario è dovuto andarci* and *Mario ha dovuto andarci*, French has *Mario a du y aller*. Finally, the clitic *y* cannot move to a position preceding the main verb, unlike Italian clitics: in French one cannot say **Mario y est dû aller*. Because of these differences, one might expect French learners to overgeneralize auxiliary *avere* as a result of L1 influence. This seems to be the case in Figures 1 and 3, but not in Figure 2, which shows a clear preference for the correct sentence with *essere*. One cannot therefore say that the French subjects are overgeneralizing *avere* across the board. Obligatory auxiliary change with clitic movement is acquired, despite the fact that French does not have clitic movement. The optionality of auxiliary change with the other two constructions, on the other hand, seems to be eliminated by the French near-natives, who reduce it to a categorical choice involving *avere*. The use of auxiliary *essere* in these constructions is overall less frequent and more marked than the use of *essere* in the present. If L1 influence plays a role at all, it is in conjunction with typological factors and markedness considerations. As for the English near-natives, what needs to be explained is why they do not seem to overgeneralize *avere*, given that this is the only auxiliary available in their L1. They do not transfer from the L1 and at the same time do not attain target-like knowledge.

Question 3

In the case of obligatory auxiliary change with clitic movement, both groups of learners have been exposed to frequent and robust evidence in the input. Only the French learners, however, seem to have 'noticed' such evidence and therefore acquired the property in question. The English learners, on the other hand, do not seem to have 'noticed' such evidence and their judgments are still indeterminate after many years of exposure. One can say that the French learners, because of the overall typological similarity between French and Italian, are in a more favourable position to notice such input than the English learners, regardless of the fact that French, like English, does not have clitic movement. The overall characteristics of the French grammar with respect to auxiliaries may also explain why they acquire a divergent representation of optional auxiliary change. Similarly, the overall characteristics of the English grammar may explain why the English learners do not acquire either a convergent or a divergent representation for any of these constructions.

Question 4
Given that some of these rules are optional, both groups of learners may use only auxiliary *avere* in their production without making any errors. The same outcome in production results from very different knowledge representations.

Question 5
Figures 4, 5 and 6 show that the responses of the two groups of near-native speakers in the card sorting task are similar to the responses of native Italians. None of the contrasts shown by the magnitude estimation task is also shown by the card sorting task.

Question 6
The difference between the task in Part 1 and the task in Part 2 is that the first task is timed, that is, it does not allow time for reflection or second thoughts, whereas the second task is untimed, that is, it allows subjects to respond at their own pace and therefore to consult their metalinguistic knowledge. The discrepancy between the results in Part 1 and those in Part 2 suggests that the timed task engages tacit knowledge, but the untimed test probably engages metalinguistic knowledge. At the metalinguistic level, both groups of subjects know the facts of the Italian grammar. It is only at the level of tacit knowledge that the differences between the two groups, and between each group and the control group, become apparent.

Additional Discussion
Further to question 1, one could point out that these constructions are more open to change, as shown by the fact that French used to have them at a previous stage of diachronic development.

Problem 3.7

Purpose: To consider the effect of semantics on syntactic acquisition and to consider L1 influence.

Data Source: Sorace, A. (1995). Acquiring argument structures in a second language: the unaccusative/unergative distinction. In L. Eubank, L. Selinker, & M. Sharwood Smith (Eds.), *The Current State of Interlanguage* (pp. 153-175). Amsterdam: John Benjamins.

Question 1
Transitive verbs are in sentences 1, 3, 6, 9, 11, 13, 17, 20.
Intransitive verbs are in sentences 2, 4, 5, 7, 8, 10, 12, 14, 15, 16, 18, 19, 21, 22, 23, 24.

All transitive verbs are used with the auxiliary *avere* 'have'. Some intransitive verbs are used with *avere* 'have'; others are used with *essere* 'be'. The intransitive verbs used with *avere* are: *ha lavorato* (10), *ha corso* (12), *ha saltato* (15), *hanno giocato* (18), *ha dormito* (19), *ha viaggiato* (22). The intransitive verbs used with *essere* are: *sono aumentate* (2), *è arrivata* (4), *sono esistiti* (5), *sono saltati* (7), *è corsa* (8), *è appartenuta* (14), *è venuta* (16), *è restata* (21), *sono sopravvissuti* (23), *è affondata* (24).

Question 2
(a) The intransitive verbs denoting an activity with no change of state/location are:
ha lavorato (10), *ha corso* (12), *ha saltato* (15), *hanno giocato* (18), *ha dormito* (19), *ha viaggiato* (23).
(b) Verbs denoting the existence of a state are: *sono esistiti* (5), *è appartenuta* (14).
(c) Verbs denoting a change of state that can also be used transitively are: *sono aumentate* (2), *è affondata* (24).
(d) Verbs denoting a change of location are: *è corsa* (in farmacia)(8), *è venuta* (16).
(e) Verbs denoting the continuation of a pre-existing state are: *è restata* (21), *sono sopravvissuti* (23).

Question 3
Unergative verbs are used with *avere*. Unaccusative verbs are used with *essere*.

Question 4

The verbs *correre* 'run' and *saltare* 'jump' are used with *avere* when they denote a physical activity with no change of location; they are used with *essere* when the sentence contains an expression that indicates a change of location (such as the phrases *in farmacia* 'to the pharmacy', and *giù dal letto* 'off the bed'). These verbs can therefore be both unergative and unaccusative, depending on the context in which they appear.

Question 5

Recall that unaccusative verbs are normally used with auxiliary *essere*. Figure 1 shows the judgments of native Italians and learners of Italian on unaccusative verbs presented with the incorrect auxiliary *avere*. Consider the judgments of native Italians, indicated by the light grey bars. Of the different semantic types of verbs, verbs of change of location are the least acceptable with *avere*; verbs that can be both unergative and unaccusative depending on the context are the most acceptable with *avere*.

Question 6

(ranging from least to most acceptable with *avere*)

Beginners:

change of location < continuation of state < existence of state < unaccusative with transitive alternant < unaccusative with unergative alternant

Intermediate:

change of location < continuation of state < unaccusative with transitive alternant < unaccusative with unergative alternant < existence of state

Advanced:

change of location < continuation of state < existence of state < unaccusative with unergative alternant < unaccusative with transitive alternant

Native speakers:

change of location < continuation of state < existence of state < unaccusative with transitive alternant < unaccusative with unergative alternant

Question 7

Figure 1 shows that not all unaccusative verbs are judged as equally unacceptable with the incorrect auxiliary *avere*. There is a hierarchy of semantic types. Verbs of change of location are the ones that are rejected most strongly when they are presented with *avere*. They are also the first verbs for which auxiliary selection is acquired by learners of Italian. Verbs of continuation of state and verbs of existence of state follow, in that order. At the opposite end of the hierarchy we find verbs that can have different meanings, and different auxiliaries, depending on the context: these verbs are judged by native speakers as the most acceptable with *avere*, and are the last ones to be acquired. Overall, there is gradual approximation of learners' judgments to the native hierarchy.

Question 8

Generally speaking, the semantic factor telicity ("change with a clear resulting state") seems to be what triggers the strongest reactions in native Italians, and also what makes verbs most salient from the point of view of second language learners. Verbs denoting continuation of state are less telic than verbs of change of location, because they imply the negation of change; and verbs denoting existence of state are not telic because they do not imply change at all. Verbs that can have more than one meaning, such as *aumentare* 'increase' and *correre* 'run' are at the bottom of the hierarchy, probably because of their variable behavior: they are not judged by native Italians as completely unacceptable with *avere*, and they are clearly the most difficult to acquire.

Question 9

The French near-native speakers judge different types of unaccusative verbs in the following order (ranging from least to most acceptable with incorrect auxiliary *avere*):

change of location < continuation of state < existence of state < unaccusative with transitive alternant < unaccusative with unergative alternant.

This order is the same as the order given by the native Italian speakers.

Question 10
The orders of acceptability for unaccusative verbs with *avere* is the same for both French and English near-native speakers of Italian, regardless of the fact that French has auxiliary selection but English does not.

Question 11
The judgments of near-native speakers of Italian are very similar to those of native Italian speakers.

Question 12
There seems to be no L1 influence with respect to the acquisition of auxiliary selection with unaccusative verbs, compared to the presence of L1 influence in the acquisition of optional and obligatory change in constructions involving modal verbs and clitic movement (Problem 3.6). One possible explanation is that the semantic parameters that govern auxiliary selection with unaccusative verbs are universal (or at least valid across typologically similar languages), and therefore constrain the grammatical development of L2 learners regardless of their language background. Another possible explanation is that the choice of auxiliary in compound tenses is facilitated by the existence of semantic parameters. On the other hand, the choice of auxiliary in constructions involving modals followed by unaccusatives, or the movement of clitic pronouns, is a purely syntactic phenomenon and therefore more difficult to acquire.

Question 13
The sentences in Part Three involve the use of auxiliary be where English allows only the auxiliary *have*.

Question 14
These verbs are intransitive verbs denoting a change of state (*happen, die*) or a change of location (*fall*). They are unaccusative in Italian and are used with the auxiliary *essere* 'be'.

Question 15
The data show a tendency in learners from very different language backgrounds to associate the auxiliary be with unaccusative verbs (particularly with verbs denoting change), even though English allows only *have*.

Additional Discussion
The strong connection between *be* and unaccusativity is confirmed by the fact that English used to have auxiliary choice at previous stages of diachronic development, and *be* was employed with the same verbs that select *essere* in modern Italian.

Problem 3.8

Purpose: To focus on 1) parametric variation, 2) notions of difference and difficulty, 3) asymmetries in the direction of difficulty, and 4) positive and negative evidence.

Data Source: Yuan, B. (1993) Long-distance and short-distance reflexives in second language acquisition. In C.S.Rhy, D.Adger & A. von Klopp (Eds.). *Functional Categories, Argument Structure and Parametric Variation* (pp. 115-147). Centre for Cognitive Science, University of Edinburgh.

Question 1
There is a clear order of difficulty for the three constructions: Chinese learners of English have the least difficulty with sentences involving local antecedents, which are grammatical in English. These sentences are recognized as acceptable at all proficiency levels. Sentences involving preverbal reflexives and long-distance antecedents, which are ungrammatical in English, elicit different judgments across proficiency levels: they are accepted initially and then increasingly rejected at higher proficiency levels.

Question 2

English learners of Chinese gradually acquire knowledge of the fact that Chinese allows both local and preverbal reflexives. However, they do not acquire knowledge of the grammaticality of long-distance reflexives, which are rejected even at the highest proficiency level.

Question 3

The asymmetry revealed by these data is surprising because one might have expected the reverse pattern. English learners of Chinese receive positive evidence in the input that long-distance reflexives are allowed in Chinese; yet, they do not 'notice' such evidence and do not acquire this property. Chinese learners of English, on the other hand, do not get any evidence of the ungrammaticality of either long-distance or preverbal reflexives, since these two constructions do not occur in this input; yet, they acquire target-like knowledge. Given that both groups are exposed to classroom instruction, negative evidence (correction and metalinguistic explanations) may play a role. It is possible that the positive evidence available to English learners of Chinese is too subtle, or infrequent, for them to notice it. It is also possible that other syntactic properties of English act as 'indirect positive evidence' in indicating to the Chinese learners of English that the binding of reflexives is much more restricted than in Chinese.

Additional Discussion

One topic that can be raised in class discussion is the possibility that Chinese learners of English are more sensitized to looking for pragmatic cues. Because English is a language that relies heavily on syntax (i.e., word order) for interpretation, other cues, such as those that are necessary for the interpretation of reflexives may be less important for them. Hence, English learners of Chinese would, as a prerequisite to learning the specific facts of the language, have to first learn that cues other than syntax are important.

Problem 3.9

Purpose: To consider the interaction between syntax and semantics in learning a second language.

Data Source: Gass, S. (1986) An interactionist approach to L2 sentence interpretation. *Studies in Second Language Acquisition*. 8.1. 19-37.

Question 1

Tell sentences: 1, 3, 4, 6, 7, 8, 10, 16, 17
Promise sentences: 2, 5, 9, 11, 12, 13, 14, 15, 18,

Question 2

The syntactic pattern is the same, but with *tell* sentences, the subject of the infinitive is the object in the matrix sentence, whereas with *promise* sentences, the subject of the matrix sentence is the subject of the infinitive.

Question 3

TELL SENTENCES

Sentence Type	Sentence Number
Human-human	17
Animate-animate	16
Inanimate-inanimate	3
Inanimate-animate	1
Inanimate-human	10
Animate-human	7
Animate-inanimate	8
Human-inanimate	6
Human-animate	4

PROMISE SENTENCES

Sentence Type	Sentence Number
Human-human	13
Animate-animate	9
Inanimate-inanimate	15
Animate-inanimate	18
Human-inanimate	11
Human-animate	14
Inanimate-animate	2
Inanimate-human	5
Animate-human	12

Question 4
In those sentences in which there is no conflict of information, the general tendency is for the correct interpretation to occur. Where there is conflicting information, semantic information (represented by the hierarchical relationships) prevails at the earlier proficiency levels. Syntax dominates at later stages.

Question 5
The results of the *promise* sentences are even more complex. Equal status promise sentences generally start out with a greater percentage of correct responses.. With some of the levels, the results get worse before they get better (see levels 3 and 4). With unequal status, but "converging" sentences, there is a tendency for the syntactic information to prevail, but not as strongly as for the *tell* sentences. For example, the correct interpretation does not take place with any consistency until level 4, whereas for the tell sentences, there was a clearer pattern for correct interpretation by level 3. Where the information diverges, both *tell* and *promise* sentences show similar patterns.

Question 6
L2 learning reflects a high degree of dependence on syntactic information. However, where there is conflicting information provided by semantic and sytactic information, semantics is given greater weight at early stages of learning with a greater reliance on syntactic inormation coming as a function of proficiency. Learning an L2 involves knowing the relative ordering of elements of a sentence (i.e., syntax) and knowing the relative importance given to syntactic information as opposed to other types of information (e.g., pragmatics, semantics).

Additional Discussion
The discussion of these data relate to studies undertaken within the framework of the Competition Model. Articles appeared in a 1987 special issue (Volume 8, issue 4) of *Applied Psycholinguistics*.

Other discussion can center on slight perturbations in the data. For example, in Table 1, the results are less clear in the inanimate-inanimate sentences than in the others.

Students can also be asked to think about what would happen with sentences that pattern like *tell* (such as *advise, order, persuade*).
Sentences with *ask* can also be discussed—for example, differences in interpretation between:
        The child asked her mother to have a cookie.
        and
        The mother asked the child to have a cookie.
The original article has data pertaining to this difference. Or students can be asked to do a mini-study themselves and ask NNSs (and NSs) for their interpretation.

Problem 3.10

Purpose: To show the effects of language universals and the interaction between universals and language transfer; to show the non-unitary nature of the acquisition of syntax (tense/aspect)

Data source: Gass, S. & Ard, J. (1984). L2 acquisition and the ontology of language universals. In W. Rutherford (Ed.)., *Second Language Acquisition and Language Universals* (pp. 33-68). Amsterdam: John Benjamins

Question 1
For the progressive, the following order can be determined:
> 9 > 2 > 6 > 3 & 4

For the simple present:
> 14 > 5 > 1 > 11 > 7

For the future:
> 8 > 10 > 12 & 13

The differential acceptability of these sentences suggests that tense/aspect is not acquired as a whole, but rather crucially depends on various meanings for the different forms.

Question 2
The data show clearly that syntax is not acquired as a unitary phenomenon. One cannot consider the acquisition of semantics without a concomitant consideration of the semantic load of various forms. Perhaps the most striking feature is the low acceptability of sentences describing states or events whose time frame is not associated with the core (basic) meaning—that is, 1) future states or events for the future; 2) present states or events for the progressive or simple present. This suggests further that the acquisition of some aspects of syntax are dependent on the semantic function of syntactic structures.

Question 3
Spanish speakers are not simply translating from Spanish and transferring the Spanish judgments for this English-based task.

Question 4
Spanish speakers appear to be basing their judgments on the core meanings of these items (which are universally determined). In other words, there is an interaction between universal and native language facts.

Question 5
For the progressive, the following order can be determined:
> 9 > 4 > 6 > > 2 > 3

For the simple present:
> 14 > 5 > 11 > 1 > 7

For the future:
> 10 > 8 > 12 > 13

Question 6
The orderings are similar, but not identical. This suggests that there are some universal constraints that govern the acquisition of these tense/aspect forms, but the differences between Spanish and Japanese also suggest an interacting factor of the native language. The major language difference is in the progressive; the present and future have virtually the same orderings.

Question 7
There is similarity in the orderings of the present and future. This suggests that universal predilections are dominant.

Question 8
There are two main points to note from these data: 1) first, one doesn't "learn" the present, or the progressive or the future. Rather, one learns the forms only together with the meanings and 2) the acquisition of the meanings is predictable based on universal core meanings; however, native language facts interact with these universal constraints.

Problem 4.1

Purpose: The focus is on phonetic interlanguage forms attributable to language transfer vs. those that are not, and the extent to which native dialect makes a difference.

Data Source: Broselow, E. (1992).Nonobvious transfer: On predicting epenthesis errors. In S.
                Gass & L. Selinker (Eds.). *Language Transfer in Language Learning* (pp. 71-
                86). Amsterdam: John Benjamins.

Question 1
Native speakers of Egyptian Arabic tend to insert an /i/ between the first and second consonants,
while native speakers of Iraqi Arabic also tend to insert an /i/ but initially in the word. In some
multisyllabic words, a similar pattern occurs but is more complicated. Egyptian Arabic speakers
insert the vowel between two consonants [d r]in the second syllable and native speakers of Iraqi
Arabic tend to insert an /i/, but in the slot [_dr] in the second syllable.

Egyptian: [tʃildiren]   children
Iraqi: [tʃilidren]   children

Question 2
Insert a vowel [i]—Egyptian after the second of the three consonants, Iraqi after the first.

Broselow formalizes the rules as follows (p. 76):

Question 3
Egyptian: 0 ---> i/CC_C
Iraqi: 0 ---> i/C_C̄C
In her article Broselow accounts for the productivity of the rule and its extension to the respective
forms for children.

Question 4
The native language rules seem to match the interlanguage for the same phenomenon and thus
language transfer is a good hypothesis in this case.

Question 5
The Egyptian-English forms:

        [izbilaʃ]   splash
        [istirit]   street
        [izbilendid]   splendid
        [iski]   ski
        [izbasyal]   special
        [istadi]   study

are different from the above in that there is an initial vowel inserted, whereas,

        [siwetar]   sweater
        [silayd]   slide

do not have such a vowel inserted but follow the native dialect rule above.
The forms for *splash, street, splendid, ski, special, study* can be accounted for according to
Broselow (p. 81) as follows: the consonant clusters in English begin in /s/ and are followed by a
stop /p/, /t/, /k/.

Question 6
If the rule is written as in question 5, then *sweater* and *slide* are not exceptions.

Question 7
These forms (*sweater* and *slide*) cannot be treated in terms of the structure of the native language.
We therefore have a case of non-transfer.

Additional Discussion
The data here directly relate to the pronunciation of English words beginning with consonant
clusters and the insertion of a vowel between them, called epenthesis. Depending on the makeup
of the class, one could investigate whether epenthesis occurs in other English interlanguages, for
example, Italian-English and how, in general, learners compensate for non-native patterns in the
target language.

Regarding language transfer, one could engage in a discussion of the comparison between phonetic and syntactic transfer: Which is more obvious, more lasting? A possible source for this discussion is an article by Ioup (1984).

Problem 4.2

Purpose: The focus is on 1) the concept of underlying forms in L2 phonology and 2) the extent to which phonological rules that learners create are natural in the sense that they are present in other languages.

Data Source: Eckman, F. (1981). On the naturalness of interlanguage phonological rules *Language Learning, 31,* 195-216.

Question 1
The alternations in these data are not entirely consistent. For example, there are cases where there is alternation [p-b]; [t-ð]; [k-g], [f-v] and cases where there is not, as in /wɛt-wɛter/. For subject 1, fricatives are voiceless in word final positions. In intervocalic position, there is a general tendency for there to be voiced obstruents. There are examples of intervocalic fricatives alternating with intervocalic stops, but there are also examples where this alternation does not occur (wɛt-wɛter). However, it is in just those examples in which "underlyingly" (see question 2), there are voiced consonants where spirantization occurs (exception is Bob-Bobby). There is also a possibility of morphophonemic alternations (-est suffixes do not condition spirantization) although there are too few examples to know this for sure.

For subject 2, there are examples of alternations (Bob-Bobby) as well as no alternations (rob-robber). There are no examples of this latter type for speaker 1. There are numerous examples of intervocalic spirantization, although, as with speaker 1, there are also examples where this alternation is not apparent. Both speakers deviate from TL norms by producing voiceless forms where the TL produces voiced forms, but not the reverse. With one exception (fuzzy), these deviations occur in word-final position. Similarly, errors in spirantization are in the same direction for both speakers. Spirants occur where stops do in standard English, but one does not find the reverse.

Question 2
Underlying forms from Eckman, p. 205 (listed in the order given in Part One)

Subject 1	Subject 2
/bɔb/	/bɔb/
/bɔbi/	/bɔbi/
/rɛd/	/rɛd/
/rɛdər/	/rɛdər/
/big/	/big/
/wɛt/	/wɛt/
/wɛtər/	/wɛtər/
/bɛd/	/bɛd/
/pɪg/	/pig/
/bigər/	/smuð/
/brev/	/smuðər/
/brevər/	/rab/
/prawd/	/rabər/
/prawdəst/	/du/
/sik/	/ridu/
/sikəst/	/bek/
/fris/	/pribek/
/son/	/sef/
/fʌasi/	/sefəst/
/ðə/	/ðə/
/faðər/	/ðis/
/tæg/	/bæd/

Question 3
Eckman suggests a rule of terminal devoicing ([-sonorant] ↳ [-voice]/_____#) and
Postvocalic Spirantization   -sonorant
$$\begin{vmatrix} -sonorant \\ +voice \end{vmatrix} \Rightarrow [+continuant]/[+syllabic]\underline{\qquad}$$

Question 4
Both speakers have examples of word final voiced obstruents apparently in free variation with word final /ə/ following voiced obstruents. This differs from the phonetics of the two speakers in Part One. These two are much more similar in their phonetics than were the Spanish speakers.

Question 5
Underlying forms from Eckman, p. 209 (listed in the order given in Part One)
Subject 1   Subject 2

Subject 1	Subject 2
/tæg/	/ænd/
/rab/	/hæd/
/hæd/	/tɔb/
/hɪz/	/staDɪd/
/smuðə/	/fiʊd/
/rayt/	/bɪg/
/dɛk/	/rɛkənayzd/
/zɪp/	/ɪz/
/mɪs/	/sɛz/
/wɛt/	/wɔtə/
/difər/	/afə/
/ovər/	/lidə/
/bigər/	
/kɪkɪn/	
/tæpɪn/	
/lebər/	
/blidɪn/	
/lidə/	

Question 6
Eckman proposes a rule of Schwa Paragoge: 0 -> ə/ -sonorant_____
                                                                    +voice
What is interesting about this rule is that it is not motivated for other languages. A rule of Schwa Paragoge is not motivated for the grammar of any language which is acquired as a first language. Eckman argues that this rule is necessary to resolve the conflict that exists between underlying representations and surface phonetic constraints. This leads to the question of whether or not interlanguages are "natural languages". One could conclude that they are not given the data presented in this problem. However, one could argue that they are in that the non-natural rule (Schwa Paragoge) is motivated by facts of the NL and the TL. The Spanish data in Part One reflect a natural rule (Final Devoicing) which is motivated in many natural languages (e.g., German).

Additional Discussion
To posit underlying forms in IL's, one must assume that the learner has some knowledge of what s/he is aiming for and that there is then a rule that takes him/her from the targeted form to the produced form. An underlying form of /wet/ vs. /red/ nicely accounts for the difference between the comparative forms of these two words for both Spanish speaking subjects. The difficulty in positing underlying forms is selecting the appropriate form. Because learners notice that there is a difference between two forms does not necessarily mean that they perceive the same difference that native speakers do. It is quite possible that what is salient for the NNS's (in this case probably native speakers as well) is the difference in vowel length and not the consonant difference. Thus, attributing a difference in underlying forms to the consonant may be misleading. On the other hand, not positing underlying forms may preclude valid explanations and ignores the fact that some patterning exists.

Problem 4.3

Purpose: To determine the relationship between production and perception.
Data Source: Sheldon, A. & Strange, W. (1982). The acquisition of /r/ and /l/ by Japanese learners of English: evidence that speech production can precede speech perception. *Applied Psycholinguistics, 3*, 243-261.

Question 1

The low-level Japanese made the greatest number of errors in identifying words. This included not only errors in their own speech, but also errors in English speakers and higher level Japanese speakers. The greatest number of errors of perception were made on the speech of the low-level Japanese. Everyone made errors based on the speech of this group.

Question 2

The production of the good Japanese appears to be quite good; there was only one perception error by native English speakers. On the other hand, they made 11 errors of perception when judging native English speakers. This suggests that their production is better than their perception.

Question 3

All three perception types (self, other good Japanese, native English speakers) seem to be more or less the same. Thus, self-perception seems to be only minimally better than perception of others.

Question 4

Self-perception in this comparison is worse than perception of native speakers: 1 error versus 17 errors (10 + 7). One could conclude that the learners don't know how good they are.

Question 5

The production of all, but #6 (poor Japanese) is good. Only #5 has 3 errors (out of 96 tokens). Subjects 1 and 2 have poor perception with numerous errors of others and of self. These two subjects, then, show better production than perception. Subjects 3-5 have reasonably good perception and production. One cannot say that either perception or production is better. Subject 6, the low-level Japanese, also has more or less equal perception and production. One would like to know if subjects 3-5 are different in proficiency levels from 1 and 2. If so, one could talk about production preceding perception as a developmental trend.

Question 6

The most difficult context for perception is different for /r/ as opposed to /l/. For /r/ the most difficult context is in consonant clusters, followed by word medial. The easiest appears to be word final position, at least in the perception of native speaker speech. For /l/ the most difficult context is word initial, followed by word medial, consonant clusters and word final position, at least in the perception of native speaker speech. The order for perception of Japanese speech, the order is similar (medial, initial, consonant cluster, final), but not identical.

Question 7

When Japanese learn English /r/ and /l/ differences, they are instructed from an articulatory perspective. That is, they learn where the place and manner of articulation are for these sounds. Without significant practice in the area of perception, the contrast will not be noticed.

Question *8

A contrastive analysis of Japanese/English predicts that Japanese will have difficulty with the /r/, /l/ contrast in English since there is only one corresponding phoneme in their NL and because there are phonetic differences between their corresponding phone and the English ones. However, contrastive analysis doesn't predict the different degrees of perceptual difficulty in the various contexts (question 6). Japanese /r/ occurs in word-initial and medial positions, but not word finally. Also, there can be no consonant clusters with /r/. Thus, one would predict that these sounds would be equally difficult in word-final position and in consonant clusters. This was not the case (question 6).

Additional Discussion
One could raise the question of the generalizability of these findings to other areas of phonology. If the explanation of pedagogical influence (question 7) is correct, this may suggest that the generalization of perception before production does not hold beyond these particular sounds for this group of learners.

Problem 4.4

Purpose: 1) To investigate production and perception of individual sounds in L2 phonological acquisition; 2) to consider the relationship of age of first exposure and ultimate attainment, and 3) to consider length of exposure and ultimate attainment.

Data Source: Flege, J.E. (1988). Factors affecting the degree of perceived foreign accent in English sentences. *Journal of the Acoustical Society of America, 84,* 70-79.

Question 1
The native English speakers rate the speech of learners who began learning English as children as less accented than the speech of learners who began learning English as adults. However, the speech of learners who were exposed to English as children is rated as more accented than the speech of native speakers. The native speakers do not perceive any significant difference between the two groups of learners who began learning English as adults in terms of accent. Taiwan-5 (the longer residence group) differentiate between native speakers, learners who had been exposed to English since childhood, and learners who had begun learning English as adults; they do not differentiate between the longer and the shorter residence groups. Taiwan-1 do not seem to perceive any difference among the groups in terms of foreign accent.

Question 2
The ability to perceive a foreign accent seem to increase with length of exposure.

Question 3
The pronunciation scores given to the two groups of learners who had started learning English as adults do not differ significantly.

Question 4
The Taiwanese learners who have resided in the US for an average of 5 years are able to distinguish native and non-native speakers better than the learners who have lived in the US for an average of 1 year. This shows that perception abilities improve with increased proficiency. Their pronunciation, however, does not significantly improve, as indicated by the fact that the two groups are rated the same by native speakers in terms of their foreign accent. Perception seems to be ahead of production (See Problem 4.3).

Question 5
The average age of first exposure of the long-term resident learners is 7.6 years. On the whole, early exposure to a foreign language does not seem to guarantee the attainment of a native accent. At least, the learners in this study had not started early enough. It is possible that the acquisition of L2 phonology depends on a very short 'sensitive period' in early childhood.

Question 6
The lack of difference between the pronunciation scores of Taiwan-1 and Taiwan-5 suggests that length of residence is not a determinant factor for the acquisition of a native-like accent if people begin learning an L2 as adults. Length of residence is a significant predictor of success in terms of L2 pronunciation only if language acquisition begins during childhood. Length of residence in adult learners does, however, have an effect on the ability to perceive L2 sounds accurately.

INTERLANGUAGE USE

In this section the problems deal with language use; hence the focus is on production data, not so much as a reflection of what learners know about the language (as in the previous section on interlanguage knowledge), but rather on how learners use language. In the section on variation, we present data that reflect the different language forms that are produced as a function of the medium used (spoken/written) and the tasks used to elicit data. We also consider the extent to which forms vary within the course of a conversation and are therefore not dependent on task type.

In the oral language section, we begin with the well-established notion that in conversations involving nonnative speakers there are numerous interruptions that occur as participants often compensate for a lack of understanding. These interruptions often take the form of questioning particular utterances [*you say there's been a lot of talk about what?*] and/or requesting conversational help [*could you spell one of those words for me?*]. In other words, they "negotiate" that which was not understood. Negotiation of meaning refers to those instances in conversation in which participants need to interrupt the flow of the conversation in order for both parties to understand what the conversation is about. In conversations with nonfluent speakers, the following conversational ploys are often used:

Comprehension check
NNS: I was born in Nagasaki. Do you know Nagasaki?
Confirmation check
NNS1: When can you go to visit me?
NNS2: visit?
Clarification request
NNS1: ...research
NNS2: research, I don't know the meaning.

In learning a second language, one must learn more than just the pronunciation, the lexical items, and the appropriate word order; one must also learn the appropriate way to use those words and sentences in the second language. For example, one must learn that within the context of a telephone conversation, "Is X there?" is more than a request for information, but is also a request to speak with that person. In fact a typical response from a child is "Yes" with no further indication that he or she will call the person to the phone. Thus, a child in learning a first language must learn to go beyond the literal meaning of utterances to understand the pragmatic force. The same can be said for second language learning and use. Consider the example below, a conversation between a British tourist and a native speaker of Finnish.

(Example provided by Maisa Martin)
Tourist: We're trying to find the railway station. Could you help us?
Finn: Yes. (full stop)

In Finnish the pragmatic force of a request for utterance does not coincide with the pragmatic force in English. Thus, despite a Finn's perfectly grammatical English, one often finds what might be interpreted as abrupt responses.

Much of the work in interlanguage pragmatics has been conducted within the framework of speech acts. Speech acts can be thought of as *functions* of language, such as complaining, thanking, apologizing, refusing, requesting, or inviting. Within this view, the minimal unit of communication is the performance of a linguistic act. All languages have a means of performing speech acts and presumably speech acts themselves are universal, yet the *form* used in specific speech acts varies from culture to culture. Thus, the study of second language speech acts is concerned with the linguistic possibilities available in languages for speech act realization and the effect of cross-cultural differences on second language performance and on the interpretation by native speakers of second language speech acts.

It is easy to imagine how miscommunication and misunderstandings occur if the form of a speech act differs from culture to culture. An example was presented earlier. Native speakers of British English and native speakers of Finnish differ in the way they ask for directions and also in the way they interpret requests for directions. When breakdowns occur, they are frequently disruptive because native speakers attribute not linguistic causes to the breakdown, but personality (individual or cultural) causes. Thus, in the example given, the British tourist is likely to have interpreted the Finnish speaker's response as rude and/or uncooperative. In this section are problems on second language pragmatics, dealing with appropriateness of forms in relation to the situation of use and the addressee.

Also included in this section are problems dealing with communication strategies. Many times a learner is faced with a need to express a concept or an idea in the second language, but finds herself without the linguistic resources to do so. A communication strategy must be employed. A communication strategy is a deliberate attempt to express meaning when faced with difficulty in the second language. Bialystok (1990) (see Problem 7.1) reported the following incident:

> While living in Colombia, a friend of mine wanted to buy some silk. The Spanish word for silk, *seda*, however, is apparently used for a variety of synthetic substitutes. Eager to have the genuine product, my friend went into the local shop and, roughly translated from Spanish, said something like the following to the shopkeeper: "It's made by little animals, for their house, and then turned into material." (p. 1)

The person described in this episode did not know an unambiguous word for *silk,* nor the word for *silkworm,* or *cocoon* and thus had to resort to various descriptive devices to get the meaning across. The use of circumlocutions, such as these, is known as communication strategy.

In dealing with the notion of communication strategies, most researchers have included three components in a definition of communication strategies: problematicity, consciousness, and intentionality. By problematicity one means that the learner, in using a communication strategy, must have first recognized that there is a problem of communication that must be overcome. Inherent in the notion of consciousness is the idea that learners must be aware that they have encountered a problem and be aware of the fact that they are, in fact, doing something to overcome that problem. Including intentionality as part of a definition of communication strategies implies that learners have control over various options and make choices about which option will result in a particular effect (Bialystok, 1990).

Problem 5.1

Purpose: To focus on generalizations that learners make in using tense in oral and written narratives. The problem also compares learners from different native language backgrounds (Arabic and Italian) on this same task.

Data Source: Original data

Question 1

Past

I saw today a movie about a man in a big city.

Present

I want to tell you about a movie, my friend.

Past

The movie began with a man about 40 years old or 45 in his apartment in the city and he was disturbed by alarm clock, TV, and noisy outside the house or outside the apartment and he woke up in a bad temper and he wanted a fresh air, he went when he opened the window to get this fresh air, he found a smoke, smoke air, dirty air. The movie also showed that the man not only disturbed in his special apartment or special house, but in everything, in work, in street, in transportation, even in the gardens and seashores.

Present

Man in the city has to wake up very early to go to the work and he has to as the movie shows, he has to use any means of transportation, car, bus, bicycle and all the streets are crowded, and he has no no choice or alternatively to use and he is busy day and night. At day, he has to work hard among the machines, the typewriters and among papers, pencils and offices in the city.

Past

And when he wanted to take a rest in his house or outside his house in the garden or the seashore....

Present

He can't because the seats are crowded with people.

Past

When he wanted to take a meal in restaurant,

Present

the restaurant is crowded, everything is crowded in the city and very, very it' s not good place or good atmosphere to to live in.

Past

The movie showed that. And the man began to feel sick and thus he wanted to consult the doctors to describe a medicine or anything for for health, but the doctors also disagreed about his illness or they couldn't diagnose his illness correctly.

Present

This they show at first. Want to make us know about the life in the city.

Past

The man began to think about to find a solution or answer for this dilemma. OK dilemma? Dilemma. He thought that why not to go to the open lands and to build houses and gardens and and to live in this new fresh land with fresh air and fresh atmosphere

Present

and why don't we stop smoking in the factories by using filters, filters and stop smoking from the cars and all industrial bad survivals or like smoking like dirty airs and so on.

Past

The man also wanted to make kids or childrens in the houses not to play or to use sports inside houses, but to go outside the houses in the garden and to play with balls, basket anything.

Present
They like to play.

Past
And also he wanted to live in a quiet and calm apartment.

Present
People inside houses must not use TV in a bad way or a noisy way. Must use it in a calm way or in a quiet way and that, I think, that is a good solution or a good answer for this city dilemma.

Students sometimes do this in columns, or use color highlighting pens to indicate the different uses of past and present.

Question 2
In general, there seem to be two overlapping interlanguage-particular ways of using tenses here; first, tense shifts seem to coincide with topic shifts and, shift from specific statements about the movie to generic statements about life in the city, for example: *The movie began* (past); *Man in the city has to wake up* (present)

These might very well be linked with article choice from *a* ➔ *the*.

Question 3
Past
I saw a movie about a man in a city (big city).

Present
I want to tell you

Past
what I saw

Present
and what is my opinion.

Past
The movie began with a man about 40 years old, in his apartment in a big city. He was disturbed by many things like Alarm O' Clock, T.V., Radio and noisy outside.

Present
He want a fresh air,

Past
but he could not

Present
because the city is not a good place for fresh air. There are many factories which fill the air with smoke.

Past
The movie showed the daily life of a man in the city.

Present
He is very busy day and night.

Past
He had to go to his work early by any means of transportation, car, bus, bicycle.

Present
The streets are crowded, everything in the city is crowded with people, the houses, streets, factories, institutions and even the seashores. Man in a big city lives a hard and unhealthy life, noisy, dirt air, crowded houses and smoke are good factors for sickness.

Past

The man in the big city tried to find answer to this dilemma. Instead of living in crowded, unhealthy places, he wanted places

Present

that must be used for living. People must live in good atmosphere climate and land. Gardens, which are good places for sports, must surround houses. My opinion is that man' s solution for the problem is good and acceptable especially for health.

Question 4

The function of tense shifts seems similar here to the that in the oral data, with the rhetorical function dimension still at work, operating in topic shifts and shifts from specific statements about the movie *(what I saw)* to generic statements *(what is my opinion...)* about life in the city. What is interestingly surprising is that there are proportionally more tense shifts in the written retelling than in the oral version. In the oral version the speaker shifts tense 15 times, while in the written 13, but the oral version contains approximately twice as much data as the written. What seems to be happening is that the function and tense shifts in the domain of retelling the movie about life in the city occur in similar places, but it is the amount of information after each instance of tense shift which differs.

Question 5

This Arabic learner's tense shifting in written discourse as opposed to oral is very similar according to rhetorical functioning, as just described, that is, the domain of discourse is more important than the activity type (here written vs. oral). What is important, and this is why there is a separate question here, is that such similarities/differences in interlanguage variation should not be assumed.

Question 6

Past

So it there was a movie, um probably filmed some years ago in Budapest . . .from . . . it was a Hungarian? a Hungarian film. It was a cartoon, and it dealt with modern life in the big city. The man who uh well the....

Present

It is a description of the life of a man in a big city. From morning when he wakes up and go to work with many other people all living in the same . . . under the same circumstances and uh with the same paternistic form in the big city. And from a very common description of life of modern life, of our pressure, of our stress, of our anxieties and of all the um possible uh limits and uh rules we have to follow living in a big city. And it deals with uh

Past

it dealt with pollution problems in a town, in a city where industry and uh residential areas are very close together.

Present

And . . . the moral of the story is uh that if people could do something all together the population would have the courage and the will to do eh something for . . . to deal with these problems that may reasonably be able to find a solution or to encourage authorities to face the problem and . . . to find solutions to the. . . to it, because it's not so difficult in fact.

Question 7

This speaker seems to be focusing much of his retelling not on the facts of the film, but on the meaning behind it. The past seems to be used both a) to set the scene (he begins the retelling by giving background information about the movie in the past tense, where it was filmed, type of movie...) and b) to summarize the specifics of the film, for example: - - *it dealt with pollution problems..*

Interestingly, this follows a false start where he begins in the present. The present here is used for both specific and generic information. Another use of the present seems to be in expressing the moral of the story: - - *and ... the moral of the story is...*

Question 8
Past
The film dealt mainly with problems concerning our modern life in a big city.

Present
The main character of the story is an ordinary man living and working in the city. The film describes his everyday life and shows him in the different moments of a typical working day. In doing this the author of the story tell us about general very common problems of a modern city, where "civilization," industrialization and the consequent need for more apartment buildings, have brought to serious damages to the environment. A city, therefore, where people do not live, but vegetate; where it is hard to find peace and loneliness; where pollution constantly endangers our health. Towards the end, however, the author suggests the possibility of finding solutions and bringing improvements to the present condition through the active participation of citizens in dealing with the matter.

Question 9
The tense shifts here are minimal. The writer begins by setting the scene in the past tense which is similar to the oral version, but then shifts to the present and stays there, dealing both with the specifics of the movie as well as general statements transcending the events of the movie. The former is seen in:- - *the film describes his everyday life and shows him in* ...whereas the latter is seen in: - - *the author of the story tell us about general and very common problems of a modern city...*

Thus, the rhetorical function shifting of the oral version shows up in the written but seems to be more 'compact'.

Question 10
First, the Arabic speaker's distinction by tense of specific/generic does not show up in the Italian speaker's versions. In the Italian oral version there still is a rhetorical patterning, but the past is used both for statements of setting and summary, whereas the present is used for both specific as well as generic statements. Accounting for this by native language transfer would not be wise at this stage; it would be better to account for it by rhetorical point of view of the speaker/writer, though native language parallel baseline data would be necessary.

Additional Discussion
This problem can be related to general issues of variation (within individuals or across individuals).

Problem 5.2

Purpose: To provide practice in analysing second language data for non-standard features in a fluent non-native speaker; to determine characteristics of early interlanguage; to analyse the difference between L1 influence and developmental processes.
Data Source: Data collected by Professor S. Pit Corder and presented to Edinburgh courses in Applied Linguistics.

Question 1
Some of the nonstandard features in this learner's interlanguage are:

subject pronouns:
- often null: /0/ is small.; /0/ is government school; /0/ can understand, yes...
- use of reduplicative or resumptive subject pronoun: Some of them they take Malay .... ; some they take two dialec...; My grandmother she speak...

morphology (person, number, tense):
- lack of 3rd person agreement: She speak...; She wear...; My father know to speak but my mother do not.; My grandmother she speak...
- expected plurals often not used: two three month back...; a group of friend...; some they take two dialec...
- gerund, present participle used in idiosyncratic ways: Around my parent staying.; So we studying...;

articles:
indefinites:
- rarely uses indefinite articles where expected: Sometimes she wear /0/ sarong.; They usually have dishes on /0/ big tray.
- indefinite seems to occur with ethnicity: I am a Teochew.; my mother a Hokien.; My other grandmother is a Baba Teochew; and with set phrases: a few; half a year; a group of...

definites: very few are used here.
- used for groups in the plural: Some of them they take Malay as one dialec'and some they take two dialec', that means the Chinese and the Malay.; Yes - mos' shop -Mos' Chinese shop - but for the Malay and the Indians I think some of them open.
- Also used idiosyncratically: Last year, due to the business I get no holiday.

word order:
- overuse of statement word order for question; inversion does not seem to exist: You ever been to China?; You know mee, ah?; you know baba?...
- topicalized in affirmatives: Very nice place is Hong Kong.; My place there I got one.

negation seems standard:
- No I am a Teochew.
- My father know to speak but my mother do not.
- I am not very sure.

Question 2
Systematicity can be decided either qualitatively, as in the use of the definite article for groups in the plural; or statistically, for example, where one expects 3rd person singular to be marked, in 75% of the cases -s is omitted. This is a stronger statistic than those cases where one expects noun-plural marking in standard English; 60% it does not appear but in 40% of the time it does.

Question 3
Many of the above would seem to be due to transfer: null subject in Chinese and lack of article in Chinese may lead to the variation seen above. Also, transfer would seem to account for insertion of reduplicative or resumptive pronoun. Developmental late acquisition of 3rd person -s may be at play here, but why it should persist may also be due to lack of equivalent NL category.

Zobl (1980) and others point out, some processes may be both language transfer AND developmentally based, thereby reinforcing each other.

Question 4
This interlanguage seems well established and according to practice, it can assume to be fossilized in at least some of the above features. However, no longitudinal data are presented, so it is impossible to state for certain that in this case, the interlanguage is unlikely to change.

Additional Discussion:
One topic worth discussing is the variable use of standard and non-standard features and what may be driving their use. Another involves fossilization, that is, how one can demonstrate its occurrence. These are particularly interesting cases where one may feel sure that this person will not change their interlanguage in the above key features. Whether explicit teaching and serious motivation to change (e.g., suddenly marrying into the target language and culture) will ever promote change leads to useful and continuing discussion.

Another topic can deal with the universality of a topic-comment stage in early interlanguage, regardless of the L1, or whether this is typical only of learners from topic-prominent language backgrounds (e.g., Chinese). It is to be noted that three of the recurrent features in the data (double subjects, no agreement, and no expletive subjects) are a characteristic cluster of properties in topic-prominent languages (Fuller & Gundel, 1987).

Problem 6.1

Purpose: To investigate what contributes to NNS comprehensibility with a focus on pronunciation and grammar.

Data Source: Gass, S. & Varonis, E. (1984). The comprehensibility of non-native speech. *Studies in Second Language Acquisition, 4,* 114-136.

Question 1
The sentences read by an individual subject consist of an ungrammatical and a grammatical counterpart: for example, sentences 1 & 23 are paired; sentences 2 & 13 are paired; sentences 3 and 12 are paired.

Question 2
In general, the grammatical version of a sentence is judged as having better pronunciation than the ungrammatical version. For example, subject number 1 read two sentences—6 and 9. In sentence 6, the ungrammatical version, his pronunciation was rated as good by 8 raters and bad by 19 raters. On the other hand, sentence 9, the grammatical version, was rated as good by 26 raters and bad by only 1 rater.

Question 3
This part is optional and may be done before questions 1 and 2. This is a way for students to see if their answers correspond to those that were obtained in the actual study (see Question 4). If divergences should occur, possible reasons can become a focus of class discussion. This could then lead to a discussion of the importance of replication in SLA research.

Question 5
For this part one could also have students do their own transcriptions of the sentences rather than using the data presented in Part Two. A number of criteria could be used. One could determine the sentences which are easiest to understand by means of a ratio of number of words correct to the total number of words in a sentence. Alternatively, one could use a syllable count. One could give partial credit for parts of words (for example in sentence 2, one could give ½ point for *ectic* as opposed to *active*).

Question 6
The ordering will depend on the actual criteria used.

Question 8
This question would only be used if students do their own transcription. Here they would compare their results to the results from Part Two.

Question 9
Those sentences that are grammatical are in general easier to understand than their ungrammatical counterparts.

Question 10
However, pronunciation interacts so that if one's pronunciation is excellent, grammaticality is less important—that is, both grammatical and ungrammatical sentencesare easy to understand (sentences 1 & 23). Similarly, if one's pronunciation is very accented, both grammatical and ungrammatical sentences will be equally difficult to understand (sentences 14 & 24).

Problem 6.2

Purpose: To consider the role of input in the use of zero pronouns.
Data Source: Gass, S., & Lakshmanan, U. (1991). Accounting for interlanguage subject pronouns. *Second Language Research, 7,* 181-203.

Question 1
The NS provides input to the NNS in the form of sentences without subject pronouns (*Ahm, is a boy*). He also confirms incorrect sentences, for example, in 1 the NS says *Is a dog,* the NNS responds with *Is a dog? Good,* to which the NS responds *Good.* It is likely that the NNS believes that he has responded correctly, in other words, that the previous sentence *is a dog* was correct. Or, in 2 (Alberto), the NNS says *No, is weekend* and the NS says *Very good, good.* There is also repetition. For example, in 5 (Alberto), the NNS says *Drink too much* and the NS repeats that. All of these examples suggest to the NNS that the forms he is using, subjectless sentences, are being approved in some way by the NS.

Question 2

In many situations, it is the NS who is initiating the incorrect utterances. This is significant in that the NNS is being led to believe through this incorrect input that these are in fact standard sentences of English.

Question 3

In Figure 1, we note that the percentage of null-subjects varies between 31 and 39% in samples 1-4. However, from sample 5 onwards there is considerable fluctuation. The highest percentage of subjectless utterances occurs in sample 11 which represents a nearly 15 point increase from the previous sample. When considering Figure 2, we see that the highest percentage of subjectless utterances in the input occurs in sample 11. This might suggest that the subjectless utterances in Alberto's speech are directly related to the speech of the NS.

Question 4

Figure 3 essentially starts with sample 3 because there was no English used in samples 1 and 2. The two graphs show similar trends with a high use of subjectless utterances at sample 3 followed by a tapering off from then on.

Question 5

As with the previous set of data, Cheo's greatest number of uses of subjectless utterances comes in precisely the sample in which there is the greatest number of subjectless utterances as input (sample 3). It is possible that his use of subjectless sentences was influenced by his NL, and that it was reinforced by the NS's confirmation through input and even initiation of subjectless sentences that this is correct English.

Additional Discussion

There has been considerable discussion in the literature about pro-drop sentences, particularly by speakers of languages that allow this phenomenon (as Spanish does) (see White, 1985 for an early example). The discussion has dealt with these sentences as evidence that learners have access to Universal Grammar. The data in this problem suggest that an explanation of UG access does not take into account the input that the learner is exposed to (in this case through interaction) and how the input might influence learner forms. In other words, UG is not the only explanation for the appearance of subjectless utterances in these Spanish speakers' interlanguages.

Problem 6.3
(A tape accompanies this problem)

Purpose: To have students analyze and consider the role of negotiation routines in SLA.
Data source: Varonis, E. & Gass, S. (1985). Non-native/non-native conversations: a model for negotiation of meaning. *Applied Linguistics, 6*, 71-90.

Question 1

This conversation is similar to a conversation between two native speakers of a language in the way turn-taking is established. It differs in that there are more comprehension checks (e.g., *more or less OK?*, *Do you understand more or less?*) and confirmation checks (*english*? *Ingress*?) than in most conversations between two native speakers or between two individuals fluent in the same language.

Question 2

Most of this conversation can be characterized as having understanding as its primary focus. That is, most of the conversation focuses on just trying to understand what the other is saying. But, the language focus in the conversation is a necessary prerequisite to the basic meaning exchange. Varonis and Gass describe non-understanding routines as: "those exchanges in which there is some overt indication that understanding between participants has not been complete" (p. 73). A further elaboration of these data can be found in Chapter 6 of Gass & Selinker (1994) and Chapter 5 of Gass (1997).

Question 3
NNS J frequently questions NNS S when a word is not understood. NNS J starts out by trying to say that her father is retired and that he used to be an accountant concerned with the income (*ingress*) of his company. However, J does not understand the key words *retire, institution, state,* and *ingress*. So from the initial nonunderstanding of *retire*, other nonunderstandings arise.

Question 4
The nonunderstandings are due in part to lack of knowledge of lexical items—for example, *retire*. In the case of the non-English lexical item *ingress*, there is an additional pronunciation complication in that the word is perceived as *English* and then *ingless*. If students listen to the tape in addition to reading the transcript, other possibilities might come up.

Question 5
There are more instances of nonunderstandings when there are two NNSs in a conversation. The least number of nonunderstandings occur when a NNS is in a conversation with a NS. One could argue that the reason there are more indications of nonunderstandings in NNS-NNS dyads is because in fact there *are* more nonunderstandings. On the other hand, one could argue that NNSs feel more comfortable in conversations with other NNSs and feel less embarrassed to ask for clarification. In other words, it is not that there *is* less understanding, but that the participants are more willing to let their interlocutor know when they have not understood. One could further argue that there is a mutually recognized "incompetence" in the domain of the L2 which provides a non-threatening forum in which to express one's "ignorance," something learners cannot easily do in conversations with NSs.

Question 6
Of the four groups there seems to be a progression from least negotiation of meaning (and possibly greatest understanding) for those groups where there is the greatest amount of shared background (language and proficiency level) and the most negotiation of meaning where there is the least shared background (no shared language and no shared proficiency level).

Additional Discussion
Much class can can focus on the role that these instances of negotiation play. The model presented in the original Varonis & Gass article can be used to diagram other conversations (see appendix) to determine the number and depth of negotiation routines.

Problem 6.4
(A tape accompanies this problem)

Purpose: To provide students with practice in transcription and analysis of non-native conversation.
Data source: Tape.

Question 1
The actual transcript for this conversation is given in Appendix I. Examples of meaning negotiation are the following:

DE: Woman has a [dɔk]
DR: Duck?
DE: Dɔk
DR: Dʌk oh I see
DE: A dɔk
DR: What kind of dog?

On his back
On his back? OK some clothes

He's barking
Barking?
ARF ARF

One could discuss the extent to which these really are negotiation routines or just echoes used as a strategy to keep the conversation from lapsing into silence while one is drawing.

Question 2

The entire conversation seems one of cooperation where both participants are intent on making themselves understood in order to accomplish the task at hand—drawing the picture. Evidence of this is using non-linguistic information to get one's ideas across, as in ARF ARF to describe barking. There are also numerous examples of backchannels (*uh huh, hm hm*) used as feedback. At one point DR tells DE that she is good at drawing.

Question 3

The beginning of a self-correction can be seen when DE says *yeah and it really funny the dog wear some clothe I mean eh* but then is interrupted with a question by DR. There is a series of article self-corrections when DR says *the dog is hm the dog's position is between man a man the man and the guy right?* Confirmation checks are frequent—*on his back?, barking?, twist?, flat shoes?* Comprehension checks are less frequent. One might want to question whether DR's comment *something like that* (two times) is a form of comprehension check, and if not, what function it serves.

The data here will depend on the tapes produced by the students.

Questions 4-6

This transcript appears in Appendix I. This differs from the transcript in Part One in that the speakers are of different language backgrounds and one is male and the other female. DE here seems less patient than in the first interaction. For example, at the beginning after DR has described the "guy", DE asks a question and basically asks DR to slow down. He says *I'm going to describe this guy to you OK?* Which could be taken as "Don't ask so many questions, I'm trying to describe". He continues by telling her how to organize the task. Similarly, later he says to her *I tell you how.* This gives an impression of lack of cooperation, although during the conversation DR seems willing to respond patiently to numerous confirmation checks. DR's comment *Now you want to paint a dog* seems somewhat direct to English speakers. There are also examples of self-correction *And the woman have...um...her he-her hair.* DR provides a comprehension check when he talks about "galgo" dogs. He says: *I don't know if y-if you know ah (galgo).*

Question 7

Answers here will depend on the actual tapes collected, but in general, it should be found that there are fewer negotiations, the tape is shorter, there are fewer pauses, and so forth.

Additional Discussion

This exercise can also be used for a discussion of transcription. It will be noted that the transcriptions given in Appendix I are not detailed. For example, there are no indications for pauses. Below is a transcription convention that can be given to students so that they can have some practice in following a convention. Discussion can focus on the need for detailed transcriptions and the purposes to which the transcriptions are going to be put.

Transcription Conventions

Intonation/Punctuation

Utterances do not begin with capital letters; normal punctuation conventions are not followed; instead, intonation (usually at the end of a clause or a phrase) is indicated as follows:
At the end of a word, phrase, or clause
?   Rising Intonation
.   Falling Intonation
,   "Nonfinal Intonation" (usually a slight rise)
No punctuation at clause end indicates transcriber uncertainty

Other

(?) or ( )	incomprehensible word or phrase
(all right)	a word or phrase within parentheses indicates that the transcriber is not certain that s/he has heard the word or phrase correctly
[	indicates overlapping speech; it begins at the point at which the overlap occurs
=	means that the utterance on one line continues without pause where the next = sign picks it up (latches)
y-	a hyphen after an initial sound indicates a false start

Ex: y- your mother is coming right?
(.)   a dot within parentheses indicates a brief pause
((laugh))   nonlinguistic occurrences such as laughter, sighs, that are not essential to
                        the analysis are enclosed within double parentheses

Because the two transcripts given for Parts One and Two differ along gender lines, the following
articles might be interesting class reading:
Pica, T., L. Holliday, N. Lewis, D. Berducci & J. Newman. (1991). Language learning through
        interaction: What role does gender play? *Studies in Second Language Acquisition, 13,*
        343-376.
Gass, S. & E. Varonis. Sex differences in NNS/NNS interactions. In D. Day (Ed.) *Talking to
        Learn* (pp. 327-351). Rowley, Mass.:Newbury House

Problem 6.5

Purpose: To consider the variable nature of foreigner talk.
Data Source: Gass, S. & Varonis, E. (1985). Variation in native speaker speech modification to
                 non-native speakers. *Studies in Second Language Acquisition, 7,* 37-57.

Question 1

The average amount repaired (after Question 3) to the NSs and the high level NNSs is similar,
whereas the average amount repaired to the low level NNS is quite a bit higher. The situation
differs for Question 7. In the case of the NSs, the amount is less than to Question 7. The
situation for NNSs is different. In the case of the high level group, the amount repaired increases,
whereas the amount repaired for the low level group on the whole decreases, although this is not
the case for each individual.

Question 2

For the NNSs, one could hypothesize that the NSs conversing with the NNSs reassessed their
initial impression of the NNSs' language abilities. Remember that those responding to the
telephone call heard two questions before question 3. We focus first on the high level NNSs.
When the NNS said "Pardon me?", this may have caused the NS on the telephone to make a
certain judgment about what the problem was—possibly a problem in hearing, not
comprehension. By later in the conversation when the NNS again said "Pardon me?", the NNS
may have been convinced that this individual was not as proficient as originally thought and
hence repaired more of the original comment. For the low level NNSs, the change was not so
uniform. For two speakers (1 & 3) the amount repaired increased considerably, whereas for
another (2) the increase was not substantial. Only for subject 4 was their considerable decrease.
In general, it appears as if the NNS is reassessing the original impression of the NNS's abilities.
Further discussion can focus on why the NS repair decreased. In general, it appears as if the NNS
is reassessing the original impression of the NNS's abilities. Further discussion can focus on why
the NS repair decreased. In general, comprehension is not a static phenomenon and the on-going
changes in comprehension result in changes in the way NSs address NNSs.

Question 3

In all of these examples, the NS after the *pardon me* tends to elaborate on his/her response. For
example, in Example 1, the NS first repeats what was said and then elaborates by bringing in an
example of bread and whole wheat. In Example 2, there is also a repetition of *stock up* and then
an elaboration of the original comment, basically describing what *stock up* means. The third
example is similar. First, there is basically a repetition followed by the edition of additional
information *We don't have steak like we used to.* Finally, in the fourth example, after repeating
the word *nitrite*, the NS gives an example of where to find nitrites and creates a topic-comment
structure. What is interesting to note is that in the part of the exchange following *pardon me*,
there are examples of hesitation *uh* which may indicate that the NS is reassessing the linguistic
situation and is trying to figure out how to rephrase to make him/herself understood.

Question 4

Table 2 shows that for both groups of NNSs, there is a differential amount of elaboration
depending on whether it took place at the beginning of the conversation (Question 3) or at the end
(Question 7). For the high level group, NSs elaborated more as the conversation progressed and
for the low level group, NSs elaborated less. This shows the variable nature of talk addressed to

NNSs and the extent to which it reflects an assessment and possibly reevaluation of the NNS's ability. The NS group remains more or less the same at Question 3 and at Question 7.

Question 5

Example	Change from	Change to
1	pronoun (*them*)	full noun phrase (*my eating habits*)
2	prepositional phrase (*with preservatives*)	a relative clause (*that have preservatives*)
3	prenominal modifier (*prepackeged food*)	A relative clause (*food that's prepackaged*)
4	ellipted speech (*cut down some....*)	a full phrasal verb with particle and gerund (*on eating*)
5	ellipted speech (no subject and auxiliary)	a fully specified subject and auxiliary (*we've*)
6	a morphological comparative (*healthier*)	a periphrastic comparative (*more healthy*). Here there is a change from more information per unit (word) to less information per word
7	an unstressed indefinite article (*a*)	a stressed numerical adjective (*one*)
8	ellipted speech of auxiliary only (*doesn't, hasn't*)	the inclusion of the verb and object (*changed them*)
9	a reduced pronoun (*'em*)	a fully specified noun phrase (*our eating habits*)
10	a cross-linguistically uncommon conjunction (*try and not eat*) which is limited in productivity (e.g., can't be used in the past--*tried and ate)	a universally more common grammatical structure (*try not to eat*)

Question 6

Table 3 shows that, similar to the data on elaboration, the NS results stay more or less the same, but the NNS results "flip-flop" so that repairs become more transparent as a function of time for the low level group and less so for the high level group. As with elaboration, this suggests a reevaluation of the NNSs' abilities as a function of time.

Additional Discussion

This problem can lead to a general discussion on conversations involving NNSs and, in particular, on the variables that might trigger foreigner talk. For example, in the data presented here, appearance, vocabulary and grammar were controlled for. Yet, there was still evidence of changing talk to NNSs. A variable seen in these data is that the NNS's comprehension of the NS's speech may be a factor in eliciting NS speech modification. The NNSs had to indicate lack of comprehension (*pardon me*) and it is this lack of comprehension that may have triggered reassessment. In sum, the way one addresses NNSs in conversation changes as a function of the NNS's ability to understand and be understood in the L2.

Problem 6.6

Purpose: To show an extended example of a conversational misunderstanding and to see how such misunderstandings arise and are perpetuated through conversational devices.

Data source: Varonis, E. & Gass, S. (1985). Miscommunication in native/non-native conversation. *Language in Society. 14*, 327-343.

Question 1

One piece of evidence for cooperative discourse is the mere fact that the conversation exists. The conversation in its entirety lasted approximately 2 ½ minutes. Each party could have hung up when they realized that there was some difficulty. In fact, the authors of the original article did try to replicate this conversation using a NS rather than a NNS. The misunderstanding did not go more than two or three exchanges at which point the conversation terminated. What is interesting in this conversation is that one reason it continued as long as it did is that the NNS gave all of the appropriate backchannels. One can look at the left hand column and see that his actual input is minimal. His contribution is primarily in the form of *uh huh, OK, hm hm, yeah*. This suggests to the NS that he has understood (although her long pauses would suggest that she was aware of the fact that he hadn't). Had there been more negotiation, the conversation would have looked very different and might have terminated with the resolution of the original misunderstanding.

Question 2
There is evidence of non-understanding—more so on the part of the NS than on the part of the NNS. The NS indicates non-understanding in line 3, has a lengthy pause before line 5. There is a long silence after line 10, in the middle of line 35, and after line 45.

Question 3
The NS provides the answer to her own question in line 5 and provides an "or-choice" question in line 7. On the other hand, despite her willingness to continue the conversation, she does little to make her speech more comprehensible. For example, she is not explicit in her references. In line 23, she introduces *he* although there is no specific mention of this individual up until this point. She uses the idiomatic expression *off hand* in line 29. She uses abbreviated forms, such as *em* (them) in line 41. In addition, although not evident from this transcript, her speech was rapid.

Question 4
It is likely that the conversation went as far as it did because there was enough common ground (and perhaps good will) to allow it to continue. The conversation had as its common ground something concerning a television. At first that was the only common ground. However, the common ground expanded in line 34 to a sales transaction concerning a TV, although at this point it is still not clear who is buying and who is selling. It isn't until the end of the conversation that the true common ground is reached, that is, that the NNS wants to buy a new television.

Question 5
The conversation can be evaluated on a number of grounds. In terms of overall understanding, it appears that the original misunderstanding was resolved at the end, but what is interesting is that just at the point of resolution, the conversation terminated. In terms of rapport, both appear polite and work toward a true understanding (particularly the NS—the NNS was most likely confused as to what was happening).

Additional Discussion
One could ask students to call a TV repair store and start the conversation as this NNS did and see how how quickly the misunderstanding gets resolved. Sources of miscommunication abound in all sorts of situations of inequality (language or otherwise). How and why this might happen can serve as a basis for class discussion.

Problem 6.7

Purpose: The focus in this problem is on non-native speech acts, in this case, compliments
                and the effect of cross-cultural differences.
Data source: Wolfson, N. (1989). *Perspectives: Sociolinguistics and TESOL*. Cambridge:
                Newbury House.

Question 1
According to Wolfson's research, replicated by others, compliments occur with very formulaic syntax and lexis, for example, only a very few positive adjectives such as: *nice, good, beautiful, pretty,* and *great*; adverbs such as: *really*; and only a few verbs such as *like* or *love*, as in:
I really like your shirt.
Your house is really beautiful.

But these data are for American English situations only and one wonders if this is true for others; (see below).

Question 2
It depends on what the purpose of one's compliment is. Is it solely a compliment? Then a *thank you* is ok. If not, see 4 below, then a simple *thank you* may shut off conversation.

Question 3
This may be useful as hypotheses but see below for the fallibility of native speaker intuition in this area.

Question 4
There are many possible functions of compliments: show appreciation, approval, solidarity but the one Wolfson discusses in depth is that it is often used by native speakers as an opening to other speech acts, especially to the establishment and negotiation of a relationship.

Question 5
The intent of the compliment in each case apparently was to get a relationship going and to further conversation.

Question 6
In each case, apparently, the nonnative speaker interpreted the compliment as purely a compliment, that is, as a positive evaluation of their accent, blouse, necklace.

Question 7
It is hard to tell without further data in the ongoing exchange, but it would seem that the conversation would then be shut off, as seen in one case where the non-native speaker actually turns and leaves. Interestingly, the data show that sometimes the NS tries again, but this seems to lead again to the closing of the conversation.

Question 8
This part may be the most interesting of Wolfson's results: the NNSs either say a perfunctory *thank you*, do not react, or reject the compliment by attempting to demonstrate modesty. The NSs either accept it with pride (*Yes, I'm proud of my son*) or, if they reject it, they give unfavorable information about the object (*it is old, cheap*) and/or they transfer the credit to someone else (*my sister bought it...*).

Question 9
As a native speaker. you probably would have thanked the person and kept the conversation going. Cross-cultural differences will inevitably surface here.

Question 10
Based on Wolfson's results, there are several functions to compliments, the most important being that it is an opener, at least by Americans, to further conversation and to negotiate a relationship. Not responding to a complilment with language that furthers the conversation reduces the opportunities for input and, therefore, for conversational practice.

Additional Discussion:
Wolfson makes the strong claim that her results are the same for other dialects of native English but it is the opinion of one of the authors (NS of American English) living in Britain that misunderstandings with speech acts occur frequently in interdialect situations in exactly this domain, with Americans at times seeming like non-native speakers. It may thus turn out that the NS/NNS dichotomy in response to compliments may not be so clear. For example, in Britain, one often hears native speakers rejecting a compliment by attempting to demonstrate modesty. That is, in general, there may very well be a continuum between interlanguage and interdialect use (cf. Selinker, 1998 and web address for data-base and class notes)
[http://www.bbk.ac.uk/Departments/AppliedLinguistics/Larry.html]

Discussion here might be useful with intuitions gained, but students should be cautioned and naturalistic ethnographic research (the source of Wolfson's data) is to be preferred. This is because of another of Wolfson's results: the strong claim (and this puts in doubt results from much pragmatic interlanguage research) that native speaker intuitions about forms used in compliments (and therefore in all speech acts?) can be inaccurate.

There is thus an important pedagogical corollary here: that it might be foolhardy for nonnative speakers to depend on native speaker intuition. Wolfson claims with impressive data (she links the consistent *thank you* in the examples above to teacher input, for example) that teachers often give wrong information to learners of English. A class project could involve gathering of compliments from learners of languages other than English and compare those with NS data from that language. For an article on compliments from a language other than language, see Nelson, El Bakary, Al Batal (1995).

Problem 6.8

Purpose: To consider ways of defining fluency; to consider the effect of speech type on fluency.

Data Source: Riggenbach, H. (1989). Nonnative fluency in dialogue versus monologue speech: A microanalytic approach. Ph.D. dissertation, UCLA, Los Angeles.

Question 1
Most of the answers to this problem vary and will be based on students' responses.

Question 2
Answers will probably include features such as pauses, number of words, number of fillers.

Question 3
The opinion monologue appears to contain more speech and fewer pauses. Students could add up the amount of pause time, or the number of words. Or they could do a gross measure of lexical sophistication.

Question 4
Answers will vary.

Question 5
Times of tapes are as follows: Subject 1, narrative, 1 minute, 30 seconds, including 18.5 pause at beginning—not on tape) opinion, 1 minute; Subject 2, narrative, 35 seconds; opinion, 1 minute.

Amount of speech/minute
        Following are the numbers of words per tape:
                Subject 1, narrative   56 words
                Subject 1, opinion   50 words
                Subject 2, narrative   85 words
                Subject 2, opinion   111 words

        These numbers are subject to qualification since one can count words in different ways. For example, is can not, one word or two? Are repetitions such as, *a boy on the, a boy on the* counted as four words or 8 words?

Hesitation
        Following are the hesitation times per tape:
                Subject 1, narrative   46.7 seconds
                Subject 1, opinion   18.9 seconds
                Subject 2, narrative   9.5 seconds
                Subject 2, opinion   25.4 seconds

Extent of vocabulary use
        Following are lists of vocabulary words per subject and per tape.

Subject 1

Narrative

a	but	his	row
and	can	is	storm
are	change	many	strongs
ask	go	not	tell
boat	go up	on	that
boy	he	policeman	the
broken	him	river	there

Opinion

and	for	is	study
at	foreign	language	that

believe	future	learn	the
can	go	least	use
country	good	my	usually
English	high	one	we
every	I	other	
example	if	school	
first	in	student	

Student 2

Narrative

a	came	my	spotted
across	catch	new	that's
after	day	of	the
an	disposal	old	threw
and	dog	one	Tim
at	excitedly	owner	to
back	Fido	pair	two
black	flabbergasted	play	wanted
boys	he	ran	was
brand	it	said	wasn't
brought	John	shoe	waste
bushes	jumping	so	were
but	looking	some	

Opinion

a	folks	no	their
active	for	nursing	them
after	grandchildren	of	they
all	happening	old	think
an	home	or	to
and	I	part	wanted
are	in	paying	what
aware	is	people	what's
be	it	place	where
cared	know	rather	with
changes	live	should	world
children	living	sons'	you
daughters'	look	staying	you're
difference	lot	taking	
don't	love	than	
families	makes	that	
feel	more	the	

Grammatical accuracy
>   Following are the grammatical inaccuracies for the subjects:

>   Subject, 1, narrative
>>   A boy on the boat (no verb)
>>   A policeman tell him
>>   So he ask him
>>   So he ask him go ther-
>>   Row the boat ???
>>   Strongs the storm (incorrect verb)
>   Subject 1, opinion
>>   I believe that every high school student learn is good
>>   We usually go foreign country future
>>   If we study foreign language we can use (no object or incomplete thought)
>>   In the school
>   Subject 2, narrative
>>   Across to some bushes

Subject 2, opinion
No grammatical errors

Repair
Subject 1, narrative
A boy on the, a boy on the (repetition)
Tell him, can tell him (correction
Go ther-, go up (word change)
Subject 1, opinion
Go, go (repetition)
In my country, Eng- in my country (repetition)
Subject 2, narrative
At a waste, at a waste (repetition)
At a pair of, at an old black shoe (different structure)
And the o- and the owner (false start)
Subject 2, opinion
None

In general, subject 2 appears to be much more fluent, as evidenced by measures of grammatical sophistication and lack of hesitation.

Question 6
Answers will vary depending on students' subjective ratings.

Question 7
Answers will vary.

Question 8
Answers will vary.

Question 9
Answers will vary.

Question 10
These responses are based on the entire dialogue.

Amount of speech/minute
253 words—this figure was calculated based on the amount of "talk time" for the NNS not including long pauses
Amount of talk
452 for NNS (50.11%) and 450 for NS (49.89%)
Hesitation
14 filled pauses (uhm)
7 unfilled pauses
22 short pauses
Turns
NNS   50
NS   45
Backchannels
NNS   8
NS   25
Questions
NNS   3 (direct); 4 (indirect)
NS   2 (direct); 4 (indirect
General comprehensibility
Answers will vary
Repair
18 examples of repair, 14 of which are repitions)

Question 11
Answers will vary.

Additional Discussion
Additional class discussion can focus on defintions of fluency in monologues versus dialoges. Are they same or different? Some of the features that can be mentioned here relating to

differences are turns, backchannels, question-asking behavior. In other words, one has to be able to carry on a conversation in addition to having the language facility (e.g., non-hesitanat speech, grammatical accuracy).

Problem 7.1

Purpose: To classify communication strategies; to consider ambiguous strategies; to determine the effectiveness of strategies.

Data Source: Bialystok, E. (1990). *Communication Strategies. A Psychological Analysis of Second-Language Use*. Oxford: Blackwell.

Question 1

The strategies represented in the data may be classified into the following broad categories:
(a) avoidance:
- message abandonment: strategies 1 to 5
(b) paraphrase:
- approximation: strategies 6 to 21
- word coinage: strategy 22
- circumlocution: strategies 23 to 60
(c) transfer:
- literal translation: strategies 61 to 68
- language switch: strategies 69 to 74

Question 2

The classification of strategies into a taxonomy (any taxonomy) poses problems of interpretation. There are different levels of analysis. For example, 'approximation', 'word coinage' and 'circumlocution' are examples of paraphrase because they are all attempts to say something in a different way. At a finer level of analysis, however, individual phrases within the same utterance could represent different strategies. For example, strategy 18 can be analyzed as consisting of two strategies: *c'est une petite machine* (approximation) and *avec des nombres* (circumlocution). Strategy 10 can be seen as consisting of three separate strategies: *c'est une sorte de, tu peux dire, chaise* (approximation), *quand tu* 'move' (language switch), and *des fois c'est sur des arbres* (circumlocution). In fact, most utterances inevitably contain more than one strategy, although perhaps the main strategy choice is the overall intention of the utterance.

Question 3

The more fine-grained a taxonomy is, the more difficult it is to analyze strategy use. It is often impossible to classify an utterance unambiguously as an example of a particular strategy rather than another. For example, it may not be easy to decide whether an unfinished sentence is an example of message abandonment; very often speakers interrupt a sentence because they lack the lexical or linguistic means to complete it, rather than because they give up their original goal. The strategy 'approximation' can take different forms, depending on whether it involves naming a superordinate set (as in 10, 11, 12, 19), or a comparison with a similar set (as in 7, 8, 9, 13, 15). But sometimes the decision to use one or the other is contingent on the speaker's syntactic choice: consider utterance 15, for example, in which the use of the analogy 'cage' depends on the use of the expression 'it's like a', indicating analogy; and compare it with utterance 19, in which the use of the superordinate 'box' partly depends on the use of the expression 'is a', indicating membership.

Identification of the strategy 'word coinage' in principle would require knowledge of whether the speaker was intending to create a new word. Utterance 22 looks like a new word, but we do not know whether the speaker was simply trying to describe the object and his attempt accidentally led to an utterance which is potentially a single word. In utterance 28, it is not inconceivable that the speaker was, in fact, trying to create a new word by modifying the English term handicapped, but since the outcome happens to be a correct word no strategic behavior can be attributed to her.

There is an ambiguity in the interpretation of utterances 63, 64, 67, in that these examples may be due to non-target syntactic knowledge, rather than to the speaker's communicative intention to apply literal translation.

Question 4

This question should generate a group discussion, as there is no definite answer. It may be useful to reiterate some crucial concepts. The primary criterion for strategy use is the existence of a communicative problem and the speaker's intention to achieve a communicative goal. Strategies should critically differ with respect to their effectiveness in achieving the original goal. In this sense, strategy distinctions are valid if they correspond to distinctions in interpretations by interlocutors.   Certain strategies, such as language switch, can only be effective if the speaker and the interlocutor share knowledge of that language.   Other strategies may be more or less effective depending on the context and on the listener.

Additional Discussion

A follow-up experiment (reported in Bialystok 1990) attempted to assess the communicative effect of four of the strategies exemplified in Part 1 (approximation, word coinage, circumlocution, and language switch,) in terms of the ability of a group of native French speakers to identify the correct objects referred to from a set of objects depicted on a display board. The mean percentage of times that the correct object was identified for each of the four strategies is as follows:

approximation	51.05%
word coinage	96.88%
circumlocution	53.38%
language switch	60.38%

It is striking that the only significant difference is between word coinage and the other three strategies. These results would seem to question the validity of the taxonomy itself.

Problem 7.2

Purpose: To understand how descriptive taxonomies of communication strategies can be reduced to a process-oriented taxonomy; to understand referential strategies; to understand linguistic vs lexical difficulties in L2 descriptions and L1-L2 differences in the use of referential strategies.

Data Source: Kellerman, E. Ammerlaan, T, Bongaerts, T. and Poulisse, N. 1990. System and hierarchy in L2 compensatory strategies. In R.C. Scarcella, E.S.Andersen, & S.D. Krashen (Eds.) *Developing Communicative Competence in a Second Language* (pp. 163-178). Rowley, MA: Newbury House.

Question 1

Task to be done in pairs.

Question 2

All the utterances are attempts to describe properties of the shapes in order to put the native speaker in a position to know what particular shape is being referred to. The process of selecting relevant properties of the object being described is a referential strategy, which can be holistic, partitive, or linear according to the particular selection of properties operated by the speaker.

Examples of holistic strategies are utterances 1, 2, 4, 5, 7, 8, 9, 10. In these utterances, the speakers describe the entire shape by associating it to a real object, or to a conventional geometric figure. An example of partitive strategy is utterance 3, in which the shape is described in terms of its smaller components. Utterances 6 and 9 are examples of linear strategies: the shape is broken into one-dimensional components (such as lines, angles, spatial relations) and is treated like a series of route directions. Utterances 11, 12, 13 cannot be analysed as single strategies—rather, they are combination of strategies. Utterance 11, for example, consists of a holistic strategy (*it's a square*) followed by a partitive strategy (*this is like two triangles*), and finally of a linear strategy (*the line where they are put together has vanished*). Last, the speaker resorts to a holistic strategy in the L1, associating the shape with a well-known brand of licorice lozenges (*it's like a "wybertje"*). Utterance 12 probably starts with an aborted attempt to use a holistic strategy; when this fails, the speaker resorts to a partitive strategy, followed by a new holistic strategy (*it's a figure like two roofs of a house put together*) and finally by a linear strategy.

Question 3

The strategy preferred by the nonnative speakers is the holistic strategy: speakers always try to describe a shape holistically, and resort to other strategies only when the holistic strategy cannot be adequately applied (for example, because of lack of lexical knowledge), or when the speaker realizes that the holistic strategy is not specific enough, and therefore not effective. Partitive and linear strategies are also ordered with respect to each other: partitive is preferred to linear. However, it is not necessary for each strategy to be applied, as long as the hierarchy is not violated.

Question 4
To be discussed within groups.

Question 5
The hierarchical order for strategy types is Holistic > Partitive > Linear. Speakers will opt for the holistic strategy, whenever they can, because it is the most compact and effective, and satisfies the principle of 'least effort'. They will opt for the partitive strategy, however, if they perceive that the holistic strategy is not applicable to the particular object that is being referred to, either because there is no conventional label available, or because there is no obvious analogy. In utterance 5, for example, it is conceivable that the speaker is aware that shape 9 does not look exactly like the letter P, so she resorts to another holistic strategy (*it has a corner*), and finally realizes that neither holistic strategies are effective. The linear strategy is the least preferred because it is the most effortful (in terms of length and complexity of the description) and - all other things being equal – the least effective.

Question 6
The strategic choice of L2 learners may be affected by lack of proficiency. L2 learners are likely to experience a tension between their desire to employ holistic strategies and the need to resort to partitive or linear strategies in order to compensate for a lack of relevant knowledge. On the other hand, L2 speakers may often produce shorter L2 descriptions than they would in their L1, because they lack the linguistic and/or syntactic knowledge to handle the description. L2 speakers may also use relatively poor or ineffective holistic strategies because they do not possess the language necessary to undertake longer descriptions. Linear strategies, in particular, are demanding in terms of both lexical and syntactic knowledge, and less proficient L2 speakers may resort to the L1 to compensate for their linguistic difficulties. Kellerman et al. suggest a three-stage characterization of L2 performance in developmental terms:

1.   Low-proficiency learners produce short descriptions in the L2 (and may frequently resort to the L1);
2.   Intermediate proficiency learners produce longer descriptions (longer than those they would produce in the L1);
3.   Advanced learners produce short L2 descriptions (virtually identical to those they would produce in the L1).

References

Birdsong, D. (1992). Ultimate attainment in second language acquisition. *Language, 68,* 706-755.

Fuller, J. & Gundel, J. (1987). Topic-prominence in interlanguage. *Language Learning, 37,* 1-17.

Gass, S. & L. Selinker (1994). Second Language Acquisition: An Introductory Course. Hillsdale, NJ: Lawrence Erlbaum Associates.

Gass, S. (1997). *Input, Interaction And The Second Language Learner.* Mahwah, NJ: Lawrence Erlbaum Associates.

Healey, S. (1998). Word Associations: towards an interlanguage semantics. MA thesis, Birkbeck College, University of London.

Ioup, G. (1984). Is there a structural foreign accent? A comparison of syntactic and phonological errors in second language acquisition. *Language Learning, 34,* 1-17

Nelson, G., El Bakary, W. & Al Batal, M. (1995). Egyptian and American compliments: Focus on second language learners. In S. Gass & J. Neu (Eds.). *Speech Acts Across Cultures* (pp. 109-128). Berlin: Mouton.

Selinker, L. (1972). Interlanguage. *International Review of Applied Linguistics, 10,* 209-231.

Selinker, L. & Lakshmanan, U. (1992). Language transfer and fossilization: The "Multiple Effects Principle". In S. Gass & L. Selinker (Eds.) *Language Transfer in Language Learning* (pp. 197-216). Amsterdam: John Benjamins.

White, L. (1985). The "pro-drop" parameter in adult second language acquisition. *Language Learning, 35,* 47-62.

Zobl, H. 1980. Developmental and transfer errors: their common bases and (possibly) differential effects on subsequent learning. TESOL Quarterly. 14: 469-79

APPENDIX I

Rough transcription of Part One, Problem 6.4

DE = Describer (Japanese, female)
DR = Drawer (Japanese, female)

DE: At first I will describe this picture. OK?
DR: OK
DE: There is two person. One is woman and
DR: uh huh
DE: One is the other is a guy   mm
DR: uh huh
DE: Mm woman is uh woman is in the left side
DR: Left side? I see   woman OK
DE: Left side woman   and uh em then opposite side   it's mean the right hand side
DR: hmhm
DE: There is a guy. The guy has an umbrella
DR: hm hm   hm hm
DR: Guy has umbrella
DE: umbrella yeah and woman ehh how can I say? woman has a [dɔk]
DR: Duck?
DE: Dɔk
DR: Dʌk oh I see
DE: A dɔk
DR: What kind of dog?
DE: I'm not sure the usual one
DR: a big one?
DE: Yeah
DR: Big one like eh most American eh one
DE: Yeah
DR: American one
DE: Hm
DR: Big one OK
DE: yeah and it really funny the dog wear some clothe I mean eh
DR: OK
DE: On his back.
DR: On his back? OK some clothes
DE: hm hm   yeah
DR: Like ah sometimes Japanese women do=
DE: =yeah=
DR: =I know
DE: that is really funny
DR: Something like what can I som-something like uh what can I say
DE: It's a kind of ornament you know. It hm it doesn't work. I mean mm even if the dog wear these clothes
DR: hm hm
DE: Um the dog can never feel the hot or
DR: Yeah I see anyway
DE: No   yeah OK=
DR: =the dog wear something
DE: yeah   and the dog face the guy
DR: hmhm
DR: Face the guy I see
DE: yeah and he bark. He's barking.
DR: Barking?
DE: ARF ARF
DR: OH
DE: Wow wow
DR: oh barking OK
DE: hm barking
DR: Barking
DE: OK bark OK anyway OK OK barking. I'm not sure.
DR: OK I see OK, OK.
DE: And then woman try to control the dog.
DR: ah I see you know I see and then I have a question about the position of that dog
DE: hm hm
DR: the dog is hm the dog's position is between man a man the man and the guy right?

```
DE:   The man and a woman not the guy sorry yeah
DR:                      uh                      OK
DE:   That's right.     Then there is one from left side about describe the position    on the
DR:              OK      and                                                                        hm hm
DE:   On left hand side there is a woman
DR:                              hm hm
DE:   and she pull   a string  of dog  and dog is between woman and guy.
DR:   hm hmOK       hm hm
DE:   and the guy wanted to protect it
DR:   Hm hm
DE:            protect himself from the dog   to to use the umbrella
DR:                      hm hm                hm hm
DE:   I see!
DE:   But the umbrella isn't open
DR:                      uh open
DE:   Isn't open
DR:   OK I see and then I have several questions. mm First, about the woman's clothes
DE:   OK woman wear the hat.
DR:    uh-huh    hm hm         Hat?
DE:              mm.  She wears coat
DR:   Hm hm Oh wait wait a minute     OK
DE:   She wears long hair   hm hm and em?
DR:   Curly hair?
DE:   No
DR:   No
DE:   Uh-eh sh-she mm her hair is twist(ed).
DR:   Twist?  not curly
DE:                  into one into one
DR:   Ah ts ts tied?
DE:   Tied yeah.
DR:   One and some ribbon or something like that.
DE:   No
DR:   No just tied.  OK OK.  Something like that
DE:                      hm hm                      hm hm
DE:   Maybe uhm this woman and also this guy are are in their middle age
DR:   Oh no
DE:   Not so youn
DR:   Ah OK anyway anyway and
DE:   Not young anyway and
DR:   Her clothes?
DE:   She wears coat          That coat has one
DR:                      wears coat
DE:   Pocket.  I can see only one pocket
DR:   Uh huh
DE:   And below the coat we can see her skirt
DR:   Hm hm
DE:   Some part.  Yes, that's right
DR:   Oh you can't you can say?
DE:   Yeah
DR:   I'm not sure.  If I I can. uh I think eh it's better for me not to see not to look at your picture.
DR:                  Yes, that's right.
DE:                          Maybe. Maybe OK  And she wear shoes
DR:   High heel or    flat shoes?
DE:                  no
DR:   Flat shoes?
DE:   Flat shoes
DR:   OK
DE:   That flat shoes had a ribbon
DR:   OK
DE:   Something like sneaker
DR:   Oh no
DE:   Flat shoes
DR:   Ribbon. You said ribbon OK anyway
DE:                                  mm string?      it has string.
DR:                                  uh huh                OK string OK
DE:   And she she she want she want to a dog, the dog to be calmed down=
DR:   =Yeah. OK OK                  hm mm
DE:   Because the dog is    bark
DR:                  uh huh
DE:   Bark?
DR:   Bark.  I see.
DE:   Then the dog's mouth is open
```

DR: Yeah and dog face face up
DE: Yes
DR: To him
DE: Right.
DR: OK and dog's eh hair hair? No [indiscern]
DE   No no hair
DR   No hair
DE: Hm hm
DR: No hair uh plain one
DE: Yeah dog's rather slim
DR: Slim rather slim dog how about dog's tail
DE: Tail is long
DR: Long and which what can I say direction?
DE: Direction?
DR: Hm hm I mean uh it is faced face up or face down
DE: Down
DR: Down OK long tail oh tail
DE: You are good at painting picture good ahh and also his ears m hm hm his ears down not up.
DR: Not up. OK
DE: hm hm. OK that's right. Right. OK and opposite to the guy there is a guy
DR: And
DE: He wears formal clothing
DR: Hm hm and how about his hat?=
DE: =He has no no hat. no hair
DR: no hat?
DR: No hair? I see. No hair. He has no hair
DE: He looks be upset upset
DR: Uh huh
DE: He has a moustache   it it a moustache? On the this part.
DR: hm hm   Yes yes
DR: OK moustache and is he fat?
DE: No almost the same as woman.
DR: It means normal size?
DE: Normal size
DR: and completely bald bald completely bald
DE: No hair
DR: No hair OK I see
DE: He wears mm bow tie.
DR: Bow tie bow tie means
DE: this way hm like ribbon
DR: Like ribbon. OK. OK
DR: And dark suit maybe
DE: Hm suit. But it's really funny why he doesn't wear pants
DR: Huh?
DE: I'm not sure
DR: What does it mean?!
DE: Because this picture because this picture is really funny. It's a kind of cartoon.
DR: Yeah I know but why doesn't he wear pants?
DE: I don't know
DR: It's impossible (laughs)

Rough transcription of Part Two, Problem 6.4

DE = Describer (Spanish, male)
DR = Drawer (Japanese, female)

DE: ...make a picture of the of one guy.
DR: One guy?
DE: Uh-huh with big nose
DR: and   top of the right side?
DE: Mmm at the right side
DR: Right side   just right side
DE: yes   uh-huh
DR: Just guy?
DE: In the middle in the middle OK in the middle in the middle
DR: right side   in the middle
DE: Right side in the middle uh
DR: one guy
DE: One guy big nose uhh have ah suit
DR: big nose
DR: Have a suit! (laughter)

DE: Have a suit
DR: I can't believe
DE: Have a suit a very be- a very beautiful suit
DR: Hm-m
DE: Have a umbrella..in the left hand. And
DR: Just a monment! Just a moment! Suit?
DE: Uh-huh. I'm going to describe this guy to you OK?
DR: Oh. I I (   )
DE: I want to describe first and l-later my my   description you're you're you're have to (picture) OK.
        Listen first.
DR: OK. Listen first. (OK)
DE: OK. Is a a guy have this guy have a big nose, have a a umbrella, ..and...uh have a tie...a
        tie...mm a tie. I don't know how to   a tie?
DR: Hm-m.
DE: And have moustache...too. Kay now
DR: OK (laughter)
DE: Uh (are there) other...this this guy is in the profile, you see a the profile of the guy. You know the front?
DR: OK.
DE: I-is the profile of the guy.
DR: Like this one?
DE: You're you're...(   )
DR: (laughter)
DE: The guy have have a big a a large legs?
DR: (laughter)
DR: Large legs?
DE: Legs.
DR: Large?
DE: Large legs?
DR: Big legs
DE: No big. Large and   large, long
DR: long
DE: Umm long umm and (thin) legs. This guy don't have hair. Don't have hair. Don't have hair.
DR: Don't have   Don't have hair?!
DE: Uh-huh. And he is fat.
DR: Fat?
DE: Hm-m. He's fat, but his legs are (sim) ah no
DR: Thin.
DE: Uh-huh. Remember have umbrella in the   have umbrella. OK.
DR: ah yea.
DR: OK.
DE: In the left...part of the of the (   )
DR: in the left
DE: You want to you want to paint a woman...and the woman have a   dog in the in the in the left hand
        and the dog is...it's in   the front of the guy and is...is...is angry...with the guy and is
DR: it who is angry?
DE: The dog.
DR: OK. (laughter)
DE: It's angry with the guy. First paint the the woman in the in the left...of the in the left
DR: uhh pardon me?
DE: First uh paint the woman in the left of the   o f the paper.
DR: OK.
DE: The woman i- have a ... the the woman have a dog in her in her right hand. OK.
DR: Right hand?
DE: Uh-huh.
DR: Dog?
DE: Uh-huh. (Isn't) Is a picture this picture is (in)   the
DR: OK
DE: profile of the the the woman is you see the profile of the   woman and the profile of the dog
        too. OK. Paint the woman. OK.
DR: OK.
DE: I tell you how
DR: Just just uh
DE: Mm the woman. No   the profile. The profile?
DR: front front side
DE: Not the front. Uh the woman have ahh...ahh...(   ) a yacket.
DR: Jacket?
DE: Uh-huh. The profile of the woman
DR: a old   woman?
DE: Mmm
DR: Or young woman?
DE: You can(t)...is no is no younger but is not too
DR: Hm   old

DE: too old. The profile of the woman. The profile ( ) the   front. No(t)...y-you can(t) see the
        front you you see the woman in the profile like a man.
DR: Like a man? Ahh!! OK.
DE: And it's in front of the man. Uhh. The woman have a...a big uhh....(sheek)
DR: Big cheek ( ) now. (laughter)
DE: And her mouth it's open.
DR: It's open?
DE: Uh-huh.
DR: OK mouth is open yeah.
DE: OK. The woman wear a hat.
DR: Wear hat.
DE: And the woman have...um...her he- her hair...have uhh mmm is   not a ponytail is a ....   umm
DR: Like you?
DE: Mm. No like me. It is a ponytail.
DR: Oh really?
DE: Mmm. Have a a (ball/bow) in her hair.
DR: A bow? Ye-OK.
DE: OK. The woman wear a yacket.
DR: Jacket.
DE: and wear ahh
DR: Jacket? Oh I I I can't
DE: Hm-m   It's like a suit.
DR: Suit.
DE: Hm-m. Is is more informal like a suit. It's not too infor   mal. Uhh the yacket have a a big pocket.
DR: Big pocket?
DE: Uh-huh in the hmmm
DR: Side
DE: In the side in the in the right side. Kay. A big pocket. The woman wear the woman wear um a dress.
DR: Dress?
DE: Hm-m. Short dress.
DR: Short?
DE: Hm-m. Not too long. This is long
DR: Hm-m.
DE: Short.
DR: Yeah short (laughter) this is long
DE: uh   the the dress   is is (too) short ( ) good.
DR: Ah but (it's hard)
DE: Kay. The hand the hand of the woman
DR: OK (one) moment. short.
DE: Uh-huh.
DR: OK
DE: And have a long legs too and (sim)
DR: Long leg and (   )
DE: not too long not too long but her the legs are (sim).   The woman is fat.
DR: Woman is fat?
DE: Yeah too.
DR: But leg is...slim
DE: yeah slim. This is comic. Is a it's like a comic.
DR: Like this one?
DE: Hm-m. The the the right hand of the woman it's extended...the right hand of the woman ar- the right arm of
        the woman are extended to
DR: dog
DE: to to the the let me see uhh to....to bring th-the dog.
DR: Hm-m.
DE: But the the right hand it's extended...extended.
DR: This o- this way?
DE: Kay. The woman wear
DR: No..(   ) woman
DE: wear   The woman wear
DR: Woman wear
DE: The woman wear a tennis shoes.
DR: Tennis shoes?
DE: Uh-huh.
DR: Oh-h. It's difficult. (laughter) T..e...n...n...i...s shoes.
DE: Uh-huh. Now you want to paint a dog. The dog's in front of the guy   and he's angry
DR: hm-m
DE: and her mouth is open and the kind of of dog I don't know if y- if you know ah (galgo)?
DR: (Galgo)?
DE: Yeah.
DR: Is kind of mmm kind of name
DE: the kind of dog. Eh (galgo) is the the dog of (run) (running) the

DR: (run)
DE: the is something like uh (galgo). Have a a long long uh mouth
DR: Long mouth
DE: Uh-huh. Long nose
DR: Hm-m. (laughter)
DE: And is is a profile too. Is not front. It's a the profile of the dog.
DR: Front of (me)?
DE: No. Profile.
DR: This way? Or this way?
DE: No is in front of the guy
DR: This   ...this way?
DE: ( ) have a a long n- long nose. The dog have a long nose.
DR: ahh!!
DR: This is ear. Long nose
DE: Uh-huh and have the mouth open.
DR: Mouth open?!
DE: Uh-huh ( ) the the dog is angry with the the
DR: OK
DE: the guy
DR: (laughter) It's stupid!
DE: Th-the dog ar- is theen.
DR: Thin?
DE: Thin. And her legs his uh its l- eh their legs their legs mmm the legs of the dog are thin too. Thin and long. Thin and long.
DR: Long? (laughter)
DE: Uh th- the dog have a....a....collier col- col   c ollar in in   her in her mmm
DR: Neck
DE: Neck. Have a black
DR: Black
DE: Black col-collar I don't know what's the name and wear the the the dog wear um in this in h- in the back of the (dog) have ah something like mmm...for example mm.... wear wear a a special uh a special dress for the dog (wear) in the back
DR: just just just
DE: Just in the back.
DR: Back.
DE: Uh-huh. Yes. And...and have a th-the this (wear) is a squares   a squares yes
DR: Stripe
DR: Squares?   Stripe?
DE: uh-huh   uh-huh stripe. A squares.
DR: Ah-h.
DE: Like a...like a...uh...uh..(British) dress. (Like this guy). Um. The woman the pocket of the woman have a button in the middle in the top. Yea. Th-the the pocket of the woman   is (   ).
DR: Is (   )?
DE: Uh-huh. Have a button. Th-the the pocket have a button
DR: Button?
DE: Hm-m
DR: In the middle?
DE: In the top
DR: Top
DE: Middle
DR: Top middle
DE: And the yacket of the woman have um a button in the in the (hand) not in the hand (   ) of the arm of the yacket have a button too. And the yacket have a button.
DR: Just one?
DE: Hm-m. Umm. Let me see what more. Ah the dress of the woman have a squares is a square dress.
DR: jacket?
DE: The dress
DR: Dress
DE: The squares uhh vertical wait vertical and horizontal lines ...make a squares.
DR: Yep.
DE: the mouthes of the mouth of the woman it's big
DR: Mouth?
DE: Uh-huh. And it's open. It's open. And the mouth of the guy is s-small and is closed.
DR: Pardon me?
DE: The mouth of the of the w- of the man it's small and closed and it's closed.
DR: ahh   OK
DE: Mmm. The eye...the eyes the eyes of woman
DR: (woman's) eyes?
DE: The the eye of the woman is closer to the to the hat and is it's it's uh (real) circle
DR: Like this?
DE: It's closer to the hat to the hat and it's a a little circle and uh
DR: En...mmm no.

DE: The the eye of the woman it's a little circle and it's closer to the (hat)
DE: little circle?
DE: Circle.
DR: Uh-huh. It's doesn't matter.
DE: And the ( ) eye of the man it's ahh circle too and it's closer to the to the to the top of the of the h- of the of
        the head of the .... of the top of the of the head. It's a   circle and it's closer to the top of the head.
DR: (laughter) circle...
DE: And is...it's ehh
DR: Ahh he looked up
DE: Eh it's up to the to the mmm I don't know how to tell you it's closer to the final of the of the head. It's mmm
        how tell you.   The man how to say? the man don't have ears.
DR: Don't have ears?!
DE: No.
DR: Oh.
DE: And eh eye of the guy it's in the...eh...it's up...up in the   in the head.
DR: Yeah.
DE: And it's a square ah square excuse me a circle yeah. And the eye of the dog it's a circle too. It's good here.
DR: Oh strange. Is it OK?
DE: It's ready. We're ready. We are ready. Ready?

Transcription from Part Three, Problem 6.4

DE   = Describer (American, female)
DR   = Drawer (American, female)

DE: OK. On the right hand side there's a man OK and he's got a really big head and very skinny legs (and he's)
DR: In the middle?
DE: Yeah.
DR: Big head, bigger than Wayne's?
DE: OK (laughter). About the same size as Wayne's but his nose is on top of his head it's like a
        cartoon picture? It's a side view.
DR: Huh?
DE: I-it's so it's the side it's the it's the profile of a   man.
DR: Oh OK.
DE: OK and his nose is pointing you know toward the middle of the page.
DR: Ohh.
DE: That way.
DR: Not on top of his head.
DE: No.(but) And uh
DR: And skinny body.
DE: No wai wai wait. He's got really skinny legs but his body is real stout.
DR: OK
DE: So...yeah, just like that. ( ) OK his legs go straight down. You have to slow down a little OK. (laughter)
        OK. Put a mousta-he's got a moustache. No, no, a moustache goes under the nose. Yeah. OK. Now   OK.
DR: Kay. Now wait   Stout body.
DE: A very   stout body.
DR: Uh-huh.
DE: Alright. Now the legs are the profile of the leg too. (so)
DR: Oh so just one.
DE: Yeah you can s- kind of see a little bit of the other one.
DR: OK. Straight down?
DE: An-   Yeah. Kay no shoes so just long   feet. Yeah. O-OK. He doesn't have toes. OK.
DR: He looks like a duck!
DE: OK he's got a bow tie on. OK kind of the profile of ( ) OK and his arm you only see one arm?
DR: Hm-m.
DE: And it's holding out on a it's there's a he's holding an umbrella.
DR: OK
DE: So the umbrella
DR: straight out?
DE: Yeah so the umbrella's on the outside of his body you know like he's holding OK
DR: Hm-m.
DE: It's one of those ( ) type umbrellas.
DR: Is the you know the loop the cane is the
DE: it's on top of   (his)
DR: OK
DE: It's pointing down. The umbrella points down.
DR: Kay. How do draw (an umbrella?)
DE: Yeah. Alright. OK. (laughter) Give him
DR: Does he have a face?
DE: give him an an eye. And....give him some lips.(laughter)

DE: Alright. Now. There's a a dog is in the middle. Alright. It's one of those real skinny   t h e those are these
        people OK there's a woman on the far left and then there's a dog and then there's this man?
DR: Hm-m.
DE: I should have told you this before but they're those English types, you know?
DR: OK
DE: So, the dog is looking at the man
DR: Hm-m
DE: And it's got it's barking at him?
DR: Hm-m
DE: And it's a real skinny it's your basic dog
DR: As big as Kira?
DE: yeah (little bit) skinnier than Kira
DR: OK
DE: And then but it's kind of it looks like it's getting get- i-it looks like the woman's pulling it back a little bit
        from attacking the man?
DR: OK so the dog is facing the man
DE: with it's mouth open, barking
DR: it's mouth open
DE: And it's got a um one of those dorky uhh .... um dog suits on
DR: Oh
DE: (Like a)
DR: This looks like a (bird, Cheryl) (laughter)
DE: Are tho- where's the   w h at is (laughter) OK we're going through (   ) OK it's tail it's
DR: Oh   (......)   Kay what about the tail?
DE: It's pointing straight down like a diagonal. yeah. What's that? OK. Now give it one of those bad um
DR: Sweater suits?
DE: yeah it just covers the the top of that's why I never used those things. Like a doormat for a like a doormat
        out of on the back of a dog? It's like a saddle.
DR: Oh OK. Does it go all the way down?
DE: Yeah just like you (   ).
DR: C-
DE: Just like that.
DR: Kay.
DE: And it's plaid. OK now give it a leash. (Whatever I say is because I don't know what that is) OK
DR: Does it have a collar on?
DE: Yeah
DR: Kay.
DE: Now draw OK maybe you should draw the w- draw the woman first.
        (laughter)
DR: OK
DE: And then draw the leash.
DR: Is the woman facing the man?
DE: OK the woman's facing the man, so you've got the opposite profile (you know)
DR: Hm-m.
DE: And um she's got a big head, same thing big head, stout   body, she's got a jacket on with a plaid skirt
        underneath. So draw like this man over there. She's got a hat on though. And she's
DR: What's the hat look like?
DE: It's the uhh it's just your basic um, like Chicago gangster type hat. Like a (   )
DR: Like Pierre?
DE: Like a who?
DR: Pierre hat? (laughter) Pepe le pieu hat. French beret?
DE: No. No. It's just a it's a classic Chicago gangster hat.
DR: I don't know what that is Cheryl.
DE: It's just it's just the just a hat with a brim and a w-when
DR: oh
DE: when you think of an   look up hat in the dictionary
DR: OK   a businessman
DE: Yeah
DR: Hat
DE: Woman
DR: Woman
DE: Yeah.
DR: OK (laughter)
DE: OK she's got hair wrapped into wai-wai wait don't draw yet.
DR: Alright.
DE: And like goes down into a bun on the nape of her neck?
DR: Kay.
DE: So it's real tight.
DR: Like kind of
DE: Well it's tight it's like pulled down toward the nape
DR: oh OK
DE: of her neck

DR: How big is the bun?

DE: Um about the size of...that guys nose. (laughter)

DE: Yeah that's pretty good Ame. OK. She's got her eye is   just under the hat?

DR: Hm-m

DE: And she's got a nose about the size of that guy's?

DR: Hm-m.

DE: And uh her mouth is...she's got a huge um Jay Leno chin (laughter) and her mouth is open just a little bit.

DR: Oh now you tell me.

DE: (You   )

DR: OK.

DE: OK.She has a coat on with a pocket? On the side right   there.

DR: OK. Buttons down the front?

DE: OK. But think of her holding out her hand with the leash

DR: OK

DE: So draw her yeah stick out and then she's going to have the leash. And then she's got a little cuff on

DR: on   the neck?

DE: No on on the jacket by the wrist.

DR: Kay.

DE: A little cuff thing and then a little cuff thing in the back I don't know what those are for (   ) like a belt.....thing

DR: Hm. Should I draw the coat or   underneath is there a skirt?

DE: Yeah she's got a plaid skirt on.

DR: Straight down?

DE: Yeah it's (just) a straight skirt, a mini-skirt for an English woman.

DR: Kay.

DE: It's not plaid it's ... yeah I guess it's plaid. But   OK but on the coat? on the back?

DR: uh-huh

DE: (You know) it's just deco- for decoration?

DR: yeah, but I don't know how to draw that.

DE: It just looks like a uh...like a belt with one button coming you can't see the whole thing.

DR: Huh?

DE: OK. OK. And now put a little button on it.

DR: This end or that end?

DE: That end. Kind of ( ) (laughter) And then   there's a button on the pocket too.

DR: Right in the middle?

DE: Yeah. OK now she's got skinny legs too. But she has shoes on that tie.

DR: Two legs?

DE: You can kind of see both.

DR: Like pumps?

DE: No. Umm

DR: (men's) shoes

DE: Men's shoes yeah definitely

DR: (   )

DE: ( ) tie.

DR: OK. (laughter)

DE: They're not stick figure legs. Can you give him some leg too? (laughter) Or can you show the other one too? Can you give him a collar?

DR: Like a lapel?

DE: Yeah and actually the bow tie should be more under the   his it should be more of a protile profile bow tie.

DR: His chin

DR: Wo- how the heck do I do that?

DE: Just give him a collar.

DR: OK

DE: What else. Oh give the dog an   oh you did. Give the dog a ( ). No. nothing. nothing.

DR: OK.

DE: Is that long enough?

DR: Well with my wizard artistry, I think we're all done. Bye.

DE: Bye.

APPENDIX II

In this part of the tape, we include a variety of data types:
    1)   reading of a word list
    2)   reading passage
    3)   picture description
    4)   oral narrative

The data come from two groups of learners:
    1)   L2 English from different L1s (two proficiency levels: Note: French has only one proficiency level)
    2)   L1 English with different target languages

We present a variety of target languages (other than English) so that students of second language acquisition whose main interest is in the acquisition of languages other than English will be able to work through a systematic set of data of the language of interest. We also include native speaker data for Tasks 3 (picture description) and 4 (oral narrative) for each of the languages represented. For both Part One and Part Two, the following questions and topics may be useful:

1.   Error analysis on oral narrative and/or picture description focusing on phonology, syntax, and/or morphology (see questions to Problem 5.2).
2.   Compare pronunciation in a variety of contexts.
3.   Compare fluency in a variety of contexts (see Problem 6.8).
4.   Compare grammatical accuracy in a variety of contexts.
5.   Consider issues of hesitancy in the reading passage. Does hesitation or "stumbling" suggest lack of knowledge? Compare the hesitation/stumbling phenomena in light of production data from the narrative and picture description tasks (see Problem 6.8).
6.   What differences do you note that may depend on the proficiency level of these learners? (Part One only)

Part One

On this part of the tape, data from the less proficient speaker is given before data from the more proficient speaker.

DATA TYPES

1.   **Word List**

language	exception
exactly	differences
context	individual
known	emphasizes
talking	English

2.   **Reading Passage**
        No language is spoken exactly the same by all speakers at all times. English is no exception. Sometimes there are differences among speakers based on the geographical area in which they grew up, sometimes we find differences based on the socioeconomic group to which individuals belong, and sometimes there are differences within individuals depending on the context in which that individual is using language. Each of these differences is known by the general term *language variety*.
        This chapter emphasizes the varieties of language use which an individual uses. Language use changes depending on (1) who is speaking, (2) who is spoken to and in some cases on (3) where the language is being used. When talking about the person who is speaking, we say the speaker and when talking about the person who is being spoken to, we say the addressee.

3.   **Picture Description**: Subjects were given the picture used in Problem 6.4 and were asked to describe it.

4.   **Oral narrative**: Each subject watched "The Pear Film" (a silent film) and was then asked to orally retell the film.

LANGUAGES USED

L2 English, L1 = French, Japanese, Korean, Spanish

ENGLISH DATA

Picture Description

OK, there's a kind of a fat old woman with a bun on (ah) on her head like towards the back of her neck, and she has a hat on her head and she's got a checkered skirt on with some tennis shoes and she's holding a leash to a dog who's barking at a bald man with a moustache and a big nose who's wearing a bowtie and he's got a black umbrella in his hand and the dog...I don't know it's kind of like one of those big dogs like kind of like a ... like a greyhound maybe I don't know. And he's got looks like a not really a saddle but maybe a sweater or something on that's got all these checkers it's just on his back. And he's got a black collar around his neck and ... the people's eyes are just circles they don't really have any pupils. And the man has a suit coat on a jacket..type...thing. And the woman's got her mouth open and the man's mouth is closed.

Oral Narrative

OK, the story starts out and they show a man and he's picking pears off a tree and he's putting them in a like a pouch around his stomach and he's up in a ladder up in a tree. And...they show that for awhile and then they show a man walk by with a goat and he looks at the pears and then he keeps going and he walks past and the guy with the pears who's picking them comes down out of the tree and takes them all out of his out of his pouch and he puts them in a basket and he's got about two baskets that are full and one's that one that is empty and he goes back up in to into the tree and is picking more fruit and a little boy comes up with a bike and he stops and he puts his bike down and he looks up in the tree to see if the man's watching him and he grabs a basket of pears and he puts them in a on the front of his bike in another basket and he rides off with the pears. And he's riding his bike along and he sees this girl rid(ing) in the opposite direction towards him so he rides towards her and she's riding towards him and they pass each other and he turns to look at her and his bike hits a rock and he falls over and the basket falls out and all the pears fall (all) over the road and so the little boy gets up and he looks at his he pulls his pant leg up and looks at his knee to see if he's hurt and he sees three boys. And there's one with blonde hair, one with dark hair and one I think with brown hair and one's playing with a paddle with a little rubber ball attached to it and he's hitting it up and down. And they look at each other for a few seconds and then the three boys come over and start picking up the pears and putting them in the basket and the little boy who um fell down got up and he brush(ed) himself off and the other boys help brush him off and they pick(ed) up his bike and put the basket in the front of his bike again and helped him get up and gave him the basket and he and then they started walking away and he started walking his bike away and the three little boys walked down the road and they see (h) where his hat had fallen off so they whistle at him and he turns around and the older boy with the paddle and the ball walked up you know walks over to him and gives him his ...his hat back and the little boy with the pears gives him three pears for giving him his hat back. So the three boys walk back walk down the road and they're eating their pears and they come up to where the um...oh wait a minute. OK, they're walking down the road and then they show the guy who's picking pears again he's climbing out of the tree down the ladder and he gets down out of the tree and he looks down at the baskets and he looks from one basket and there's one empty basket and one full basket and he looks back and forth towards the baskets and then he (l-) he moves over and he sits down on the ladder and he scratch(es) his head trying to figure out what happened to the other basket and the three boys walked between him and the baskets and they're all eating pears and so he looks at them and he watches them walk away and he looks down at the baskets and looks at the guy the kids with the pears and he looks at his basket(s) again and he's trying to figure out what happened to his pears.

LEARNER DATA

Transcripts of picture description and oral narrative.

L2 English, L1 French

Picture Description

Um. I see a man, a dog, and an no I see a woman, a dog, and another man. And...the man uh look like Scottish man uhh....and uh (that is) and similarly between two mens um the dog um want to bite the a-another man. Um. The first man no the first woman the first woman is wearing the hat. Um. The second man uhh has that an umbrella. And um....the woman is um as toward as the man. The woman is speaking; the man don't speak. Um. The...the dog is between the woman and the man. Ahhh he look it it look uh angry. About the man. Um. I think the man don't appreciate the dog. Um. I don't know if this woman know this man. Um. Perhaps they want to talk but they have problem with this dog. Because this dog is not quiet. And. I'll stop.

Oral Narrative

Mm. I think um this uh story um about uh a young guy ahh he is ahh he is um making a bike ride and...and um perhaps I think this story um (prove prove) and perhaps uh he know uh the man in the tree and perhaps he help this man to bring the fruit to the village. I think the season is the summer. And. First, we we we saw uh (the/a) man in the tree he take fr-fruit. Second, we see uh another man with a an animal; he was walking um was walking and then um ahh one guy come came came and picked up pick up picked up um the fruit. And and this young guy was riding when he met ahh well when he met ah another girl riding and he had he had a problem he felt on the bottom no on the floor on the floor. No on the ground on the ground. Ahh and there were three young guys and these guys ahh help him to pick up. After that um the ahh um ....the guy was not hurt. And he gave three fruit the fruit fruit um to the three guys. It's difficult to to give a topic to this history. But um .... ok after that and um...the three guys ahh met the old man under the tree and the old man look at the three guys perhaps he's perhaps he suspect the three guys perhaps he look at the three guys he look he normally look at the three guys. OK. That's the end of the story.

L2 English, L1 Japanese (lower proficiency)

Picture Description

This this picture has one man, one dog, one woman. The man has umbrella and he has (bill) and then he has no hair. And then this woman has hat, and she has dog. She has no her dog will will will be bite this man I don't know. This dog looks like upset or something. And then mmmm like ah she looks like...funny or something. And then the man looks at nothing. Mmmm. She has shoes but ah....the man doesn't have shoes no. And the man has necktie. And the...mm. The ok. So her dog....is white oh all of them white except umbrella or something I don't know. Well, that's it.

Oral Narrative

In the morning the old man uhh take p- some pear maybe he's a farmer. And then he hmm he uh he take he take uh many pears in the ba- in the baggage or something like that. And then he he he will take a pear some pears to (again). And then some mmm a-another (old man) come come to through the his come to come to the here with a cow or (   ) animal. And so the...in in in front of the in front of the farmer's (man) I don't know exactly. And then some (   ) show the boys come to the and farmer and the farmers (no). A man (I don't know) i--s--ss is a really small boys come over here lide to bicycle. He he he steal the a lot of pears and then he reft. Then he uhh a boy a boy met a lady. So I don't know thinking about that. The man's no boy's thinking maybe this boy's really really worried and...I don't know worried and st- wo- I don't know I have no idea. And then so he no-no the the boy dumped and pear out...the bicycle. And then and then many pears and drop out to the on the ....road. S-ss. Another three boy saw this problem. So they are help to ...no...another...no-no...They help they helped they helped (together) him. And then he no uhh a 1- a boy and three boys and leave each other I don't know. So...a- uh sorry. A boy (so) lost his hat. And another boy saw see the- he he was find this hat. And then he he tell about the is this your hat or something but he never talk talked no- he didn't talk any mo- anything so I mean I think. And finally so a boy this boys (who) stole the apple pear a boy uhh give it to the four or five pears from three boys. Finally three boys walking through the farmer. This farmer is take uhh a lot of pear. So. And then three boys eating the pears maybe so this farmer saw that this situation. And I think(s) this farmer thinking about these three people three boys stealed my pears. That's it.

L2 ENGLISH, L1 JAPANESE (HIGHER PROFICIENCY)

Picture Description

There is a one gentleman and one female uhh standing. Uhh. In this paper so and the female uhh have a dog has a dog. The dog is barking to that man. I think uhh ... the the male(man?) standing has a a umbrel umbrella so the the dog ... is afraid of eh the umbrella. Because the man the man uh may hit hit him bite uh bite uh the umbrella. But the female ...keep the dog from uhh (ought to) keep him from dog. The female uhh put the ... the hat on and uhh ... wear the the jacket ... and wear the wear the skirt. yea. And ohh the dog uhh wear the... uhhh .. I don't know what the dog wear wear but uhh and the dog wear the clothes on his on his back. And. And the man uhh ... tie.

Oral Narrative

I try I try to talk about uhh this uhh movie's story. Um I saw the man have picking a the fruits up pick up the fruits. And um ... he he (keep) he keeped uhh picking up the picking up the fruits. Mmm. ... And then the a boy uhh come to here ... and ... um he... maybe helped him to he come to carry the ... fruit. And he parked his bicycle in the front of the tree a tree which is the farmer uh picking were picking the fruits. And...the the boy umm took off with bicycle and he he looked the he looked the a basket of the a fruit maybe I don't kn- I don't know the the name of the fruit exactly the anyway the a boy pick up ahh lift up the the a basket of fruit and th-he carry or put put put put the fruit on the the front of ahh bicycle and he ... he went he went to ride the bicycle. And he ehh ... he were going to uhh a boy's house uhh and on the way on the way to his house he looked at a girl who are riding the bicycle. After the ... inters-interse-intersect uhh each other bicycle the a boy uhh glanced at girl because maybe he were he was interest in the girl. Uhh and then he he hit a small rock um on riding and his bicycle hit on the rock and the boy fall fell down on the ground and ehh a basket of a fruit is scattered around ehh around the the ground. And he hit the ... the knee a knee of a knee uh maybe yea right knee and he rubbed he rubbed the the knee by his hand. At that time there's three boys appeared and then two of them helped him and ... helped pick the the fru- these fruits into the basket. And one boy ehh played (with) a toy but the two of them uhh uhh the two of them helped helped him. And...they finish to help uhh a just these boys leave ... left left and and then one of uhh the boys uhh find out the the one uhh the second hat straw hat and uhh the the one of them picked pi- picked it up pick it up and he come to hand it to a boy who riding the bicycle... and....a boy who riding a bicycle get ehh the apples to them for tha-for thanks. And .. next thing were three boys were walking uhh across the tree which the farmer uhh were picking the fruit. The ... the farmer came down came down from the tree and h-he...he wondered the .... (why the) apple why apple uhh one of the baskets of one basket of apple uhh ... is was uhh why have the basket of apples disappeared. Then he is ... he mmm he was thinking about that and ... and thinking about that the three men uhh to walk walk across the the u- the u- und- ah under the tree eh and he (   ) the boy had a the one apple on their on their hands on their hand. Uhhh. That's all.

L2 ENGLISH, L1 KOREAN (LOWER PROFICIENCY)

Picture Description

A woman take a dog with a (bite). Uh she the tried on cap and she tried on a coat. And (   ) striped shirt. And she ta- eh try on uhh shoes. And she's she's dog is uhh she's dog is now is um she's dog is 'wow-wow' now. And opposite area a man stand. The man has skin head, and has beard and he got a umbrella one umbrella and no shoes. And he take ahh emm button fly Levi's. Last dog has sweater. Strip sweater.

Oral Narrative

This (   ) silence movie. A man a man uhh catch the pear at in the afternoon. Uhh. Place is ah country. And when he catch the pear a man passed a that road with a deer. And after few minute a boy ride the bicycle uhh passed the road and he a boy ... a boy (seeked) many pears so a boy want got a pears. So he stealing a bunch of pears. He a boys ride the bicycle with the many pears. The time opposite road a girl ride the bicycle. Uhh. The time a boy's bicycle and girl's bicycle take accident. So the boy's spilled the all pears and he uhh uhh (   ) off his cap. The time uhh three three guys uhh saw see that see the situation they three guys helped uh to him for (   ) the pears. And .. the three guys uh saw see the uhh stealing boy's cap and he give the cap to boys and boys give the give some p- pears to three guys. And they depart from ... and ... and the farmer uh (that) catch the pears the farmer knows his pears uhh lost. The time three guys passed the road with ahh his pears.

L2 ENGLISH, L1 KOREAN (HIGHER PROFICIENCY)

Picture Description

Um. There are a woman and a man and a dog. A woman has a dog..uh which bite to the bite to the man. And the woman he wear a hat and wear a skirt and the man is standing in front of the dog. He has umbrella and just standing in front of the dog. Uhh. In the picture there is no moving but the dog only the dog is biting/barking toward the man. Mmm. And the man he is bored he isn't mmm...and...strangely he has no he doesn't wear shoes. And the man and woman watch watch each other. Yea. They are looking looking for each other. Mmm. And in middle the woman and the dog and then the the man is standing. I think the woman is speaking something to the man and the man just listening to her and while they are talking the dog become angry, so dog is mm biting/barking a little yea the dog seems a little violently a little dangerous yea that's all.

Oral Narrative

In the morning a farmer worked his apple tree and harvest I'm not sure this is the ( ) word but however. He harvest his apples. Eh... and while he harvest he is harvest harvesting the apples there eh a goat passed with his ... a man with a goat passed the tree and uhh...I think the h- the farmer he is very...take take care of the apples yea he well he loves the apples uhh ( ) A boy ... with a bicycle he passed the apple tree but ... uh.. he saw that the farmer is very busy harvesting his apples so he s- the boy want to steal the fruits the apples so yea he did. Ehh. But of course he is very a little scared of being caught by the farmer so he uhh he went the bicycle so fast and uhh on the way he went to his on the way he met a girl. But he pretend ahh no-no he ignored the girl and then ... uhh suddenly he fall down because of a rock on the way. So the apples spread over the road. Ah but three boys helped him. One of them have a a toy yea. They helped him so the boy who stole the apples can mmm could go to his way go on his way. Ahh but ahh one of the boys who helped him ahh pick up his hat so the boy who stole the apples appreciate about that so he gave them some apples. And...the boys who helped the boy (laughter) I know it's a little confused but however. Ahh the three boys they ahh they g- they went their way eating the apples and they pass the apple trees and the farmer saw them but of course he is not sure that ah yea before they go they went the apple trees the farmer noticed that ahh there is one apple tree basket basket missed. So he thought about that. At that time the three boys passed the way no-no-no passed ... uhh the farmer and the apple trees eating the apples. But of course the farmer can't tell them ask them about the apples because he is not sure if the apples they are if the apples which they are eating are his or not. So he just wonder about that. And the movie, the movie?, yea the movie then over at that time.

L2 ENGLISH, L1 SPANISH (LOWER PROFICIENCY)

Picture Description

There a woman and a man. The woman has a hat on the head; she has uh the hair tied. She she's with her mouth open like talking to the guy uh she has a jacket with the pocket. (   ) on her sleeve. Um well she has skirt. With lines, line cross lines and she's using sport sport shoes and she has a dog. Yea she has a dog. The dog the dog is barking. Yea the dog is barking and he has like uh I don't know how to say that but I think like, it's a kind of sweater, dog sweater(s), I don't know how to say that (laughter). And the dog is bar-yea it's barking to the guy. Ah no guy I'm sorry man and this man has um a suit a kind of yea smoking smoking. And with a black umbrella in the hand. He has a moustache. (I cannot   ). Well uh the man is not using a tie he's using a bow and the woman is not talking to this man. The woman is trying to shut the up ( ) the dog ( ) the dog is barking to the person.

Oral Narrative

OK at the beginning there's a guy hanging from a tree no hanging ( ) he was (whatever) and he was picking up uh pears from the tree and he was like a farmer a kind of farmer or something like that. Then he he went down to this ( ) he put all the pears into the ....bag...( ) he wears bag I don't know how to say it but a kind of bag and he put all the pears into this place and then uhh well....he come to to his work taking the pears from the tree (in the) pick of this tree and uhh (laughter) a little boy uh he was in in in the bic- on the bicycle. And he saw the pears and he stopped here and he stole the bag with all of these ... big the big one with a lot of pears and he put on the bicycle so uhh and he he go in his way. And the other way he he pass a a girl on bicycle too and he look at her and there was there there there was a stone and he couldn't see the stone so he fell down with the bicycle with the bag with all pears and. Three boys, there are three boys. They they they they they (looking/walking) they saw what happened and they went to help the little boy. So they pick up the bicycle and all the pears they put all the pears in in the bag and then they put the bag on the bicycle again and.....after he ( ) the way he the little boy, take the bicycle at this time he was walking and and he forgot the the the hat on the floor the land and uh one of the three these these uh three boys take the hat pi- pick the hat up and and ( ) him uh one of these boys when one one little boy was and take him the hat they gave the hat and the little boy um gave to this (boy) another little boy (laughter) um three pears so that this little boy...they they were walking eating...eating these these pears and then the the the farmers...he he goes down again and he could see that there were just two bags one empty and the other ok the other was it was full but um he just look and there wasn't any more. The other full bag. And after that, uh, he just still looking and he put he put his bag on the tree and the three little boys that helped the other one...pass him eating the three the three pears. Mmm. And he acts like he couldn't understand it I don't know why.

L2 ENGLISH, L1 SPANISH (HIGHER PROFICIENCY)

Picture Description

There is a man ... with an umbrella on the left hand. He has a tie. Uhh. He has moustache. Looks like the inspector in the Pink Panther. In front of him it's a a g- a woman with a dog. The dog was um has a ring uhh on the neck. The woman is wearing kind of jacket. Mm. And maybe a skirt or a shirts. Ehh. And then a very funny pair of shoes. She's wearing a hat and uhh. He's using a ... a funny uh hair style.

Oral Narrative

Well the story begins uhh with a man who who is behind a bushes. And uhh he's picking up he's picking pears and uhh after that uhh I realize that that bushes were in fact he was climb-uh climbing a tree. He pick uhh some pears and uhh he goes down from the tree and take those pears from from a bag and he drop it into a ba- into a basket. Then he go uhh he climbs again to the tree he goes ehh up to the tree and a man with a goat crosses in front of the pear the pears. Ehh after that, they are mixing scenes with this man picking up the tr- the pears and uhh a kid who is eh coming closer to that eh to that man in the tree in a bike r- I mean riding on a bike. The kid stops right in front of uhh in front of the baskets with the pears and uhh he notice that the man uhh on the tree is uhh distracted so he stole one of the baskets full of pears. He ride on the bike with the basket and he run away from the place. Eh he's running away and uh he notice that there is a uhh uhhh a girl that is (on)coming oncoming traffic as you can say eh in another bike ehh and when she crosses in front of him, he gets a little bit distracted. And eh he turns around and uhh the wind blows her his his hat. And after that he crashed ehh he strikes the bike eh against a rock and he fell down to the floor. All the pears are all around the place. And that happened in front of a bunch of kids. The (h-) the kids saw that and help him to put the pears inside of ( ) basket, and help him ehh help him ehh to to ride again on on the bike. So the kid is is leaving and eh suddenly th- another kid ehh whistle him and uhh give him his hat. So the other the kid with the pears the basket of pears uhh he give him eh three pears, one for each kid. And these three kids are biting the pears and eating eating and crossed exactly in fact in front of a of a guy who picked the pears from tree, but by that time that guy noticed that ehh someone stole one of a baskets. And he was wondering why ehh wou- why em those kids cross in front of him ehh eating those pears. And that's it.

Part Two

In this section, the following languages are used:

L1 English, L2 = French, German, Italian, Japanese, Spanish

On the tape (and following) we first present the native speaker baseline data followed by the L2 data. On the tape only the picture descriptions and oral narratives are given for native speakers; additionally, the Japanese and Spanish data only include picture descriptions and oral narratives.

FRENCH

Word List

villes	les étudiants
habitent	universitaire
librairies	côté
bizarre	fonda
étaient	nom

Passage

En France, les universités anciennes sont dans les villes. Les étudiants habitent, en général, près des Facultés. Le quartier universitaire est toujours très animé avec ses restaurants, ses cafés, ses librairies, ses cinémas et ses galeries d'art. Marion étudie la philosophie à la Sorbonne, à l'Université de Paris. Elle habite à côté de sa Faculté dans le Quartier latin. Quel nom bizarre pour un quartier! Quand on fonda la Sorbonne en 1257, les cours étaient en latin. Voilà l'origine du nom. Alain est étudiant en physique à Grenoble. Son université est moderne et elle n'est pas en ville. Le campus est très grand. Le campus moderne, isolé de la ville, est un phénomène récent en France.

Picture Description (NS)

Une femme qui porte un chapeau, une veste et une jupe tient un chien en laisse; le chien aboie devant un homme qui porte un parapluie, un noeud papillon et une moustache. La femme et l'homme se font face.

Picture Description (NNS)

Il y a une grande femme avec un chien. La femme porte un chapeau, une robe et chaussures, je pense la femme est vieux aussi. Son chien est faché et son chien ouvre son bouche. Il y a aussi un homme, un homme avait peur du chien, et le homme porte une (...)

Oral Narrative (NS)

L'histoire se passe à la campagne dans un pré. Un homme cueille des poires et les place dans un panier. Pendant qu'il cueille les poires, un autre homme passe avec une chèvre. Quelques minutes plus tard, un petit garçon passe en vélo, s'arrête au pied du poirier et vole le panier plein de poires. Il le place à l'avant de son vélo et continue son chemin. Il rencontre une petite fille qui vient dans le sens inverse, en vélo également. La regardant, il entre en collision et tombe. Toutes les poires sont par terre. A ce moment, il rencontre un groupe de petits garçons de son âge qui l'aident à ramasser les poires et à remettre son vélo en marche. L'homme qui cueille les poires descend de l'arbre et s'aperçoit qu'il lui manque un panier. Il compte les poires et s'aperçoit qu'il en manque. Le groupe de petits garçons passe en jouant et continue son chemin.

Oral Narrative (NNS)

Le film ouvré avec ses paysages. Il y a un homme qui collectionné les fruits et... il collectionné les fruits. Il y a un homme avec une animaux et une jeune homme dans une bicyclette. Le jeune homme prend le fruit du homme et le jeune homme fait de la bicyclette dans la rue. Le jeune homme voit une petite fille et il sourie. La petite fille mais... elle (perd) son chapeau et elle tombé et le fuit tombé aussi mais il y a trois enfants qui assisté le homme et assisté le homme...le homme continue avec ses fruits et une homme dans son chapeau et le homme donne ses fruits. Les trois enfants se promené dans la rue et passé a le grand homme qui est fâché parce que il ne voit pas ses baskets de(s) fruits.

GERMAN

Word List

beginnt	Spätgotik
berühmten	grössten
Künstler	Stilepoche
stammend	Werke
schönstes	Szenen

Passage

Die Skulptur beginnt mit dem Relief, aus dem sich erst langsam die Rundplastik entwickelt. Vor Beginn der Spätgotik, am Ende des 14. Jahrhunderts, findet man in der Malerei und Plastik nur sehr selten Werke, die mehr als historisches Interesse haben, wie etwa den berühmten Bamberger Reiter oder die herrlichen Stifterfiguren vom Naumburger Dom. Die beiden grössten Künstler dieser Stilepoche sind Tilman Riemenschneider und Veit Stoss, beide aus Franken stammend, die neben anderen Arbeiten die herrlichsten Werke geschnitzt haben. Riemenschneiders schönstes Werk ist der Marienaltar in der Creglinger Herrgottskirche, eine virtuose Schnitzarbeit, die die Himmelfahrt der Gottesmutter und Szenen aus ihrem Leben darstellt. Viele andere Skulpturen befinden sich in seiner Heimatstadt Würzburg.

Picture Description (NS)

Male zwei Personen, die sich gegenseitig angucken. Auf dem Bild ist links eine Frau, rechts ein Mann, beide gucken sich also in die Augen, man sieht sie von der Seite. Zwischen den beiden steht ein Hund und der Hund schaut den Mann an. Wenn man also auf das Bild schaut steht links eine Frau, rechts ein Mann, zwischen den beiden steht ein Hund, der den Mann anbellt. Der hat also den Mund offen. Der Hund ist eine Art Windhund, ziemlich dünn, hochbeinig, meinem langen Schwanz und trägt ein wie so ein kleines Jäckchen, hat so eine Decke auf dem Rücken und ein Halsband. Und eine Leine, die Leine wird gehalten von der Frau. Die Frau sieht aus wie eine ältere Frau mit einem Dutt, hat einen Hut auf, einen ziemlich grobes Gesicht, spitze Nase und eine Art Anorak mit einer großen Tasche an der Seite. Man sieht also von der Frau nur die Seitenansicht, das heißt, uhm und sie trägt einen relative kurzen Rock und Schuhe mit Schnürsenkeln. Ihr gegenüber, auf der rechten Seite des Bildes, ist der Mann. Der Mann hat keine Haare, kahlköpfig, einen ziemlich großen Kopf in Proportion zu dem Körper, auch eine ziemlich große Nase. Er trägt einen Regenschirm, um den Hals trägt er eine Fliege. Er hat so etwas ähnliches an wie ein Jackett aber man sieht keine Hosen, also es sieht praktisch aus wie ein Kleid. Und man sieht auch keine Schuhe, es geht einfach nur so gerade runter als wären es seine Füße. Und den Regenschirm hält er in der linken Hand, die rechte Hand sieht man nicht weil es eine Seitenansicht ist. Die Frau hält die Hundeleine in der rechten Hand und die hat einen ausgestreckten Arm und man sieht auch ihren linken Arm nicht weil es eben auch eine Seitenansicht ist.

Picture Description (NNS)

Wir haben eine picture mit zwei Leute und eine Hund und die Frau hast eine Hund mit eine, uh fehlen dieses, ich weiß nicht dieses und der Hund ist (laughter) nah dem Mann. Und der Mann hat einen oh, ich was ist der Mann hat. Der Mann sind ist nahe der Hund und der Hund oh je ich weiß nicht dieses. Von der links ist eine Frau und die Frau hat einen Hut und nicht in Seite, in Mitte ist einen Hund und rechts ist einen Mann. Und das ist alles, ich kann nicht sehen alles.

Oral Narrative (NS)

In der Geschichte geht es also um Birnen. Und die Birnen werden behandelt wie etwas wertvolles. Die erste Szene sieht man einen Mann in einem Baum sitzen und der pflückt die

Birnen, jede Birne einzeln und legt sie einzeln in seine Korb. Und das ganze sieht also sehr mühevoll aus. Er hat dann einen Korb voll, geht vom Baum runter, stellt den vollen Korb unten hin und macht sich dann langsam wieder auf den Weg wieder den Baum hochzugehen. Als er oben im Baum wieder ist, kommt jemand mit einer Ziege vorbei, geht einmal in die eine Richtung vorbei, kommt dann wieder zurück mit der Ziege und irgendwie scheint das überhaupt nicht relevant zu sein für die Geschichte. Ein bißchen später der andere, der ältere Mann, so ungefähr 40 so rum, 40, 45 sitzt also immer noch in dem Baum, kommt en Junge vorbei; so 10, 12 Jahre alt mit einem Fahrrad. Der Junge sieht sich also die Birnen an und setzt den Korb mit den Birnen vorne an seine Lenkstange und fährt los. Und er fährt und fährt und fährt also über so einen steinigen Weg und es kommt ihm ein Mädchen, auch auf dem Fahrrad, entgegen. Und natürlich, als er an ihr vorbei fährt dreht er sich um und guckt ihr nach. In dem Moment rennt er mit dem Fahrrad gegen einen Stein und fällt natürlich hin. Die ganzen Birnen rollen über die Straße. Und dann kommen drei andere Jungs vorbei und helfen ihm - ach so und bevor er beor er hinfliegt verliert er auch noch seinen Hut. Der fliegt weg. Es kommen dann drei andere Jungs vorbei. Die helfen ihm, die scheinen nur zufällig in der Gegend zu sein. Die helfen ihm die Birnen wieder in den Korb zu laden. Der Junge fährt wieder los, die drei Jungs gehen weiter ihren eigen Weg und -ah- sehen aber dann den Hut, rufen den Jungen wieder zurück, beziehungsweise gehen dann zu dem Jungen hin, geben ihm den Hut. Und -uhm- der Junge, wahrscheinlich zum Dank oder was auch immer, gibt den drei Jungs jedem eine Birne. Sie nehmen also die Birnen und jeder geht seines Weges. Und die drei Jungs gehen also weiter und kommen an dem Baum vorbei auf dem der Mann noch sitzt und die Birnen pflückt. Und der Mann kommt gerade von dem Baum runter und sieht, daß einer von seinen beiden Körben mit Birnen verschwunden ist. Und er sieht den Jungen nach und die Jungen gehen ihres Weges und der Mann sieht einfach nur den Jungen hinterher. Das ist die Geschichte -uh- ach so, das war eine Geschichte ohne Ton.

Oral Narrative (NNS)

Die sind eine man, ein Mann und ein Mann ( ) ein Frucht. Diese Mann einen Bauer und dieses Bauer. Und der Mann hat viel fruit und drei basket fruit. Und der Mann mit der Frucht und eine anderes Mann mit eine uhm animal gehen geht uhm bei den Bauern. Und dann einen Kindern kommt mit eine was ist eine, ich vergesse die Wort, mit eine cicle, bycicle, cicle,.. dieses und ein Stück no ein basket dieses Kindern bringt. Und dieses Kindern, Kinder das Kinder mit eine basket und Frucht in der basket gehen aus von dem Bauern und fährt an den Straße und ein Mädchen on eine cicle von der anderes Weg war gern und der kleine Kindern sehen dieses Mädchen und von der cicle gefällt gefällt. Und dieses basket und dieses und der Frucht on the ground gefällt. Und der Kindern also ge- gefällt. Und dann drei junge Männer kommt und dieses Kinder helfen dieses Kinder und der basket und der Frucht und die drei Kinder in der basket die Frucht uhm macht. Ich weiß nicht dieses Wort. Und dieses Kinder mit der basket von der drei Kindern gibt ein Stück Frucht und der drei Kindern fährt zu den Bauer und der Bauer sehen dieses Frucht und hat eine Frage wo geht die Frucht und uh das ist alles.

ITALIAN

Word List

pancia	fondamentali
invece	dominio
vuole	equilibrati
adattamento	muscolatura
fabbisogno	patologie

Passage

"Dormire da re", cioè a pancia in su, è una delle quattro fondamentali posizioni per dormire e in termini psicoanalitici signifca senso di sicurezza e di forte personalità. Chi dorme invece a pancia sotto rivela il bisogno intenso di mantenere il contatto e il dominio del mondo, non ama sorprese e vuole stare al riparo. C'è poi la posizione fetale che indica insicurezza e bisogno d'affetto. E infine la posizione sul fianco, semi-fetale, detta del "saggio" che rivela esseri umani equilibrati in perfetto adattamento con il mondo esterno. E anche la posizione che permette il rilassamento di tutta la muscolatura. In ogni caso, durante la notte si cambia posizione almeno 30 volte. Va anche detto che è errata l'idea che i bambini debbano dormire dieci ore, gli adulti otto e gli anziani sei. Ogni organismo ha il suo fabbisogno di riposo e quando il corpo si sveglia è inutile tenerlo a letto più a lungo o usare pillole per addormentarlo ancora, vuol dire che si è riposato abbastanza. Naturalmente questo vale in assenza di particolari patologie. In ogni caso, indipendentemente dalle posizioni derivate dalla propria personalità, molto poi dipende dal tipo di letto, dalla sua comodità, dalla sua unione con il nostro corpo.

Picture Description (NS)

Questa foto ci sono due persone e un cane. La prima persona è una signora cui quale mantiene il cane legato perchè questo cane vuole mordere all'altro signore nella foto. Questo è un cane, una specie di cane, un galgo. La signora la quale mantiene il cane è vestita col cappello, ha una giacca, ha i capelli legati, e la bocca aperta. Il signore in fronte a questo cane, mantiene un ombrello. Anche lui ha una giacca con una piccola cravatta. Il cane, questo galgo, ha la bocca aperta perchè vuol dimostrare che lui sta abbaiando. La signora mantiene il cane colla mano destra e il signore mantiene l'ombrello colla mano sinistra. Questa giacca che ha la signora ha un taschino nella parte posteriore della giacca.

Picture Description (NNS)

A questo fume ci sono due persone e un cane. La donna porta una gonna colle scarpe tennis poi una cappelle e uomo ha un ombrella. Poi il cane mi sembra come un po arrabbiata.

Oral Narrative (NS)

Questo film parla di un contadino che sta raccogliendo delle pere sopra l'albero e dopo lui scende dall'albero per una scala e mette mette tutt- queste pere in cestino. Dopo lui risale sopra l'albero e comincia riprendere altre pere. Nel frattempo questo contadino raccoglie delle pere, un bambino sta passeggiando colla sua bicicletta vicino dove sono le pere. E mentre lui passa dove sono le pere, si ferma e prende e prende questo cestino colle pere e se la porta via. Mentre lui se ne va col ces- colla bicicleta e le pere nella strada lui incontra una ragazza la quale anche lei va colla sua bicicletta passeggiando e quando lei- loro si incontrano, il cappello del bambino vola e lui si gira a guardare la ragazza e il cappello-- e scontra e la bicicletta si scontra con- contra una pietra e cade per terra con tutte le pere. Dove lui cade per terra, ci sono altri tre bambini i quali stanno giocando e vanno a aiutare a questo ragazzo. Tra- -bambini raccolgono tutte le pere le mettono- le rimettono nel cestino e poi aiutano al bambino a riprendere la bicicletta e l'aiutano andare. Quando il bambino se ne va colla bicicletta, un un ragazzo lo fischia e gli fa vedere il cappello e gli riporta il cappello. Quando gli riporta il cappello, il ragazzo il bambino colle pere prende tre pere e glieli dà questo ragazzo. Questo ragazzo se ne ritorna e gliene dà ciascuna ai suoi amici. Dopo il bambino colla bicicletta continua la sua strada e gli altri tre bambini se ne vanno camminando per il prato. Quando il contadino scende dall'albero per la scala per rimettere le pere raccolte, lui se ne accorge che gli manca un cestino colle altre pere. Mentre lui sta lì a pensare vengono camminando i tre bambini mangiando le pere. E lui rimane sorpreso dico perchè lui ha perso le altre pere. Lui immagina che questi bambini le hanno prese.

Oral Narrative (NNS)

Questo film inizia con un uomo che raccoglie delle pere dell'albero. Poi sono de pere e quando l'uomo sta nell'albero, un' altro uomo con un animali animale cammina via e non prende niente delle pere. Poi un ( ) minuti fa dopo, c'é un'altro, un piccolino un ( ) che passa via e invece lui prende tutte le pere. Dopo quando l'uomo sta ancora nell'albero, il bambino va via con le pere. Poi il bambino il bambino vede un'altra ragazza che passa via colla bicicletta e lui cade con tutte le pere. Tre bambini aiu-aiutat.. aiutano il bambino e prende gli il cappello. Lui dà il tre bambini tre pere. Poi l.. i bambini vanno via e si si passano l'uomo nell'albero. E lui vede che tutte hanno una pera nel mano.

JAPANESE

Picture Description (NS)

えー、まず絵の中に二人の人がいます。えー、左に女性右に男性がいます。えー、女性は、犬を連れています。えー、犬が、あのううん、縄を首についた縄をひっぱて男性に向かって　ほえています。あー、体をぬりだしてほえてます。えー、その紐女性が引っぱているところです。えー、女性はうんー、帽子をかぶっていて　えー、髪をうしろに一つにしばっています。えー、この女性は、えー、ポケットのついたコートをきては、あのとう登場人物は、二人とも横向きに別かれています。えー、女性の方は、うん、チェックのスカートをはいていてうん、多分ストッキングにひもぐつをはいています。えー、男性の方にうつるとえー、男性は、えー、髪がなくて頭がはげていて、で鼻の鼻の下にひげがあります。えー、この男性は、あー、スーツの上着を着ていますが、この絵によればえー、ズボンを、かいはいていないかのように描がれています。で男性はえー、ズボンをはいてなくて　靴下もはいていなくて靴もはいていません。男性は、うん、左手に　えー、傘閉じた傘をもっています。えー、とさらに　えー、男性は蝶ネクタイをしています。

Picture Description (NNS)

さあ、あの右の方は男の人、あのお友達の前で手に傘があります。あー、それね、左の所あの女の人がいます。うんー、スカート、ジャケット、あの女の人はあの犬が犬が　うん、います。　あります。うん、えーと、犬は男の人にワンワンと言ている。うん、あっ！おの人はあのお帽子を何と言うか、あの頭の上にあります。あー、男の人はあの鼻の下、あのあー、何と言う髪の毛があります。何と言うmustacheがあります。ネクタイもあります。あの女の人の髪の毛は、あのあのー、何と（（笑う））ああん何と言うか、頭のあ、あー、前じゃない、あの前の反対です。あーの髪の毛がbun，bunがあります。えーと、犬が何か、うん、しらない。

Oral Narrative (NS)

えー、始めに　うんーと、なしのような果物を収穫しているの男の人が、出て来ます。でえー、あ、この男の人が、はしごをおりていて　えー、収穫した果物をおけの大きいおけの中に入れるんですが、うんと　この男は、首に赤いバンドがまいていて　えー、白いエプロンをしていて、その白いエプロンのポケットの中にあー、収穫した果物が、あー、入いてます。でそのポケットに入いた果物を一つ一つ取り出して　あー、おけの中に入れていきますー。いきました。あー、その時に　えー、首にまいて赤いバンドがはずして　えー、収穫した果物ふきながら　えー、入れていたと思います。で（です）その果物の全部あのポケットに入いてた果物の全部入れてしまうと　再びはしごを登てあの木の上にあった実を取って、行くんですが、うんーと、男が木登ったところで別のえー、山羊をつれた別の男が、通りはかります。でこの男は、えー、おけの中に入った果物ちょっと眺めるんだけれども　えー、何にもせずにそのままを通りすぎます。えー、そのあとこんどは自転車に乗った男の子が、えー、同じ場所にやってきます。えー、この男の子は、自転車を止めると　えー、すでに　あー、収穫した果物がいっぱいになった　あー、大きなおけを自転車の前の荷台のようなところにすえつけて　えー、そのま、走して行きます。ではして行くところで　えー、男の子は正面からあー、これもやはり自転車に乗った女の子と、すれ違うんですが、すれ違う時にうん、男の子の帽子が、飛んでしまって　でその飛んでしまった帽子に気気をとられて気を取られた瞬間　えー、男の子は　前にあった何かに　えー、つまずいて　ま自転自転車の前輪が、えー、道にあった何かにぶつかって　えー、ころんでしまいます。でまー、かごはおっこて中身がころがってしまて　えー、男の子もころんでどうやらひざにけがをしたようです。での女の子自転車乗った女の子そのまま行ってしまうんですが　えー、男の子顔を上げるとそこに三人の　えー、男の子たちが立ていて　この男の子たちが男の子のおとしてしまった果物を拾うの手伝てくれます。でえー、全部かごに果物を　えー、入れると　あーの、男の子自転車に乗った方の男の子　あー、またあー、走り出すんだけれども　えー、反対方向にさって行く三人の男の子のうち一人が、道に　えー、落ちた帽子を見つけて　えー、それを自転車に乗った男の子の方に　あのう届けてあげます。えー、で　うん、ねー、そその帽子を渡したあと　えー、三人の男の子たちが、また男の自転車に乗った男の子きた方向へ　えー、歩いて行くんだけれども　うん、なぜかどこで拾たか分からないけれども、三人ともなしを持ってなしを食べながら　えー、自転車に乗った男の子が、来た方向へ帰て行きます。帰て行きますというか　歩いていきます。でこの三人の男の子が、えー、自転車に乗った男の子が、うんー、なーなしのかごを乗せた　えー、例のはじめの男の人が、なしを収穫している場所まで来るんですが。その時、えー、なしを収穫していた男の人は木からおりて　うんえーか、自分がなしを収穫したかごを眺めているんだけれど、えー、二つあるかごのうち一つは、なしがいっぱい何だけど　もう一つ

は、からぽになているので　えー、不思議そうなそうな顔をして眺めている。
えー、こーうん、これから判断するとあのなしを持って自転車で持って行った男
の子は、なしを盗んでしまったんでしょうか。ちょっと分かりませんがうん。で
えー、そこへ　えー、さき、さっきの三人の男の子が通りかかっかるんだけれど
も　うん、ふしぎそうの男の顔をした男の前を　えー、なしを食べながら三人が
通りすぎて終わり。

Oral Narrative (NNS)

あの、最初にあの男の人はにしんの木にいます。あのあの、にしが沢山あります
が木の下に　あー、うん、バスケット何と言うかバスケット、あー、にしをあそ
こね、うん、にあります。その後で　あのー、誰が男の人とどう言う動物が分か
らないけど（あうお）、木の下に歩いています。その後で、あのう、男の子、う
ん、自転車が使っている男の子が、あー、にしを見ます。えーと、自転車を止め
ます。うん、にしんを自転車の上に持ちます。その後で、また自転車　あー、を
使えます。にちの（（笑う））何と言うか、ｐｒｅｐｏｓｉｔｉｏｎか、分から
ないけど、えーとあー、自転車使っています。えー、その後であの女の子見える
自転車が使っている女の子見える。男の子と女の子が、あのー（（笑う））、ま
あパスします。男の子の帽子は、あー、頭の上にありません。その後で、エット
あー、男の子の自転車か、えー、医者医者と　あーえっと（（笑う））、ａｃｃ
ｉｄｅｎｔがあります。えーと、男の子男の子の足がちょっと痛くなると思いま
す。うんあー、一生懸命に一生懸命じゃない、えとうん、よく、あー、足を見る
ことですが、あのにしは道にあります。すぐ、あー、三人の遊んでいる男の子が
見ます。あー、そんー、その男の子たち、あーあー、自転車が使ってた男の子に
手伝います、うんえっとあー！またまた自転車の上ににしんがあります。あー、
また自転車を使えます。でもその三人の男の子が、あー、自転車を使っている男
の子の帽子見えてます。で、あー、自転車使っている男の子に、うんー　に
あー！よー呼んでいます。呼んでた。えーとあー、自転車を使ている男の子があ
りがとうのために三つのにしんを、あー、その三人にあげます。そのその後で、
また　あのう、にしんの木にいた男の人見えた。あーえっとー、（（たまいきが
つく））あー！また木の下にいた、うんー、そのあー、自転車を使ってた男の人
男の子のにし見えなかったからちょっと、あー、どこにいったかどこにあるかと
思てったと見った。えとうんあー！三人のおそんだ男の子見て　その男の子がに
しんを食べてったから、あー、男の人が、うん、何だろかと思てたでしょう。

SPANISH

Picture Description (NS)

Esta es la lámina... es el dibujo... en el dibujo puedo ver un hombre... eh... y una mujer. El hombre está a la derecha, la mujer está a la izquierda. Los dos están de pie. Umm... la mujer tiene el pelo recogido en un rodete y usa sombrero. Lleva puesto un saco con una traba atrás, otra en la manga y un bolsillo con una pliegue. Está... usa pollera a cuadros y zapatos abotinados. La señora.. eh... está sosteniendo... lleva un perro, bastante grande. El perro está ladrando al señor que está a la derecha de la lámina -la señora está a la izquierda. El perro tiene una manta y un collar. El señor es calvo, tiene bigote. Umm... lleva un paraguas que lo está sosteniendo hacia adelante. Tiene una corbata moñito..y... y... no se le ven zapatos o pantalones.

Picture Description (NNS)

Pués, hay una mujer con el perro y...hay otra hombre... ummm...La mujer lleva... una sombrera...umm... una chaqueta y falda... zapatos. El pelo de la mujer...umm...umm...es lacio...umm... El perro... umm... está gritando al hombre. Y el perro lleva algo, pero yo no se qué es... umm... El hombre tiene una corbata pero no es larga; es... umm... es... muy corto, es un *bowtie*, y está trayendo una... umm... no recuerdo la palabra, pero... umm... es para... para... la lluvia... para no sacar la lluvia... y... umm... el hombre no tiene pantalones; es muy extraño, no? No tiene zapatos también y... umm... el perro... no le gusta al hombre, en mi opinion. Y... umm... la mujer tiene un.. umm... un *leash*... no se la palabra en español, pero..umm. el perro es suya... no... y suyo..y. umm... La mujer parecía como ella está diciendo algo pero no se... umm... Bueno es todo.

Oral Narrative (NS)

En este video se ve... empieza con un señor que está subido a una escalera umm... recogiendo fruta... umm... peras exactamente y las va poniendo mientras está en el árbol subido en la escalera, arriba, las va poniendo en su delantal. Luego baja de la escalera y pone las peras en un canasto que tenía el pie del árbol. El hombre usa... está usando un pañuelo... rojo... en la cara... eh... medio estilo bandolero... aunque está bajado, no le cubre la cara. Y en un momento, después de que baja del árbol y las pone, las, las peras en el canasto, la limpia una... se saca el pañuelo, ese pañuelo y limpia una de las peras. Mientras todo esto sucede se oye un ruido afuera... umm... umm... a lo lejos y... un ruido que yo no podía identificar. Y luego cuando el señor vuelve a subir a la escalera se viene acercando un hombre... que está tirando de una... una cabra. Así que probablemente... eh... era la cabra que gritaba. Era ese el sonido que se oía atrás. El hombre pasa por delante del árb... por debajo del árbol. Este... pero no se miran, ni se hablan, no se dicen... eh... absolutamente nada. Luego viene un chico en bicicleta... y... y para, al pie del árbol. Mira las peras y agarra uno de los canastos, que tenía peras y lo sube a la bicicleta y se va. El hombre parece que no lo oye, no lo ve tampoco y el chico se va. Y... y va ca... va... umm... montado en su biccleta a lo largo de una carretera y en ese momento viene una chica, en contra. Y en ese momento que se cruzan, el chico la mira y... el viento le vuela el sombrero y él pega contra una puer... contra una piedra. Se cae de la bicicleta y todas las, las peras se desparraman. Pareciera que se lastimó en una pierna, el chico al caer, porque se levanta el pantalón y parece que tiene dolor, en... en la pierna. Umm... en ese momento aparecen tres, otros tres chicos que se acercan y le ayudan a recoger las peras, poner las peras en el canasto y subir el canasto a la bicicleta. Luego de que... de que... ponen el canasto en la bicicleta, eh... los chicos se van, los tres chicos se van... eh... en dirección contraria a la que va el chico en bicicleta. Eh... se alejan unos metros y uno de los chicos, uno de los tres chicos que le ayudaron a recoger las peras... eh... se da cuenta que el sombrero... que el... que el chico no había recogido el sombrero. Entonces lo llama, le chifla, y se acerca para entregarle el sombrero y en ese momento el chico que llevaba las peras, le da tres peras, aparentemente como... en... en agradecimiento por haberle, por haberle, por haberlo llamado y dado el sombrero. Umm... después enfocan al señor que estaba recogiendo las peras... eh... se baja...del... del árbol... y... y se da cuenta, pareciera que se da cuenta en ese momento se da cuenta que le falta uno de los cans... que debiera tener mas canastos o mas peras de las que tiene.

Oral Narrative (NNS)

En la película había una.. un hombre que había tomando las frutas de un árbol de muchos árboles realmente y umm... la fruta umm... la fruta que se llama *pear* en inglés pero olvidé la palabra español y un chico... umm... venía a... a... lugar que umm... ese hombre estuvo y emm... mientras el hombre estaba umm... en un or... árbol el chico tomó un baskete o... no se la palabra de las frutas y umm... montó su bicicleta y umm... salió umm... sin el hombre supiendo que ocurrió y umm... mientras el chico umm... estaba montando el... la bicicleta umm... miró a una chica que estaba montando una bicicleta también y umm... ella no se... se pasó a él y él trató a mirar ella y umm... umm... había una roca en frente de él pero no vio a esto porque había tratando ver a la chica y umm... el chico se cayó y las frutas se caen también; el chico le duela a la pierna y umm... y el sombrero de chico... del chico umm... se cayó también... umm... entonces algunos chicos que... que tenían umm... que tienen.. que tenían los mismos años que el chico, más o menos, ayudaban al chico y umm... y ponían todas la frutas detrás ( ) yeah detrás en el baskete para él y él... pero era un poquito extraño... pero la película fue silento y no... los chicos no... no decían nada y no decían gracias o estás bien o nada y umm... el chico montaba su bicicleta otra vez y umm... los tres otros chicos umm... pues había una chica también pero... umm... no.. no disaba que el chico no tomó el sombrero que estaba en el suelo umm... umm... Por eso umm... el chico umm, el chico que umm... que era más alto umm... trató a sacar la atención del... del chico... el chico que se cayó y umm.. y hizo un señal no se... umm... que se llama *whistle* en inglés y ummm le.. le dió... a le dió el sombrero al chico y... y... umm... el chico salió otra vez.